The Pattern
Companion:
Scroll
Saw

The Pattern Companion: Scroll Saw

Edited by Cassia B. Farkas
from material by
Dirk Boelman, Kerry Shirts & Patrick Spielman

Sterling Publishing Co., Inc.
New York

Library of Congress Cataloging-in-Publication Data Available

The Pattern companion : scroll saw / edited by Cassia B. Farkas ; from material by Dirk
  Boelman, Kerry Shirts & Patrick Spielman.
     p. cm.
   ISBN 1-4027-1269-3 (pbk.)
   1. Jig saws. 2. Woodwork--Patterns. I. Title: Scroll saw. II. Farkas, Cassia B. III.
  Boelman, Dirk. IV. Shirts, Kerry. V. Spielman, Patrick E.

  TT186.P38 2004
  745.51'3--dc22

                                                                        2004045220

2   4   6   8   10   9   7   5   3   1

Material in this collection was adapted from:
Decorative & Ornamental Scroll Saw Patterns, by Patrick Spielman & Dirk Boelman
© 2000, Patrick Spielman & Dirk Boelman
Scroll Saw Art, by Patrick Spielman & Kerry Shirts © 2000, Chapelle Ltd.
Scroll Saw Segmentation, by Patrick Spielman © 2000, Chapelle Ltd.

Detailed rights information on page 192.

It is not permitted to make the designs contained herein by laser, water jet,
CNC routers, engravers, or any other forms of high-volume production equipment.
Copying patterns to give, trade, or sell is a violation of copyright.

Edited by Cassia B. Farkas
Book design by Liz Trovato
Cover design by Alan Carr

Published by Sterling Publishing Co., Inc.
387 Park Avenue South, New York, NY 10016
© 2004, Sterling Publishing Co., Inc.
Distributed in Canada by Sterling Publishing
c/o Canadian Manda Group, One Atlantic Avenue, Suite 105
Toronto, Ontario, Canada M6K 3E7
Distributed in Great Britain and Europe by Chris Lloyd at Orca Book
Services, Stanley House, Fleets Lane, Poole BH15 3AJ, England
Distributed in Australia by Capricorn Link (Australia) Pty. Ltd.
P.O. Box 704, Windsor, NSW 2756, Australia

Manufactured in China
All rights reserved

Sterling ISBN 1-4027-1269-3

Contents

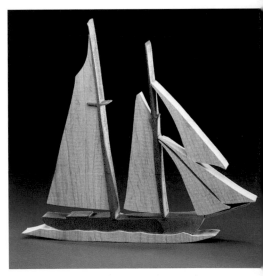
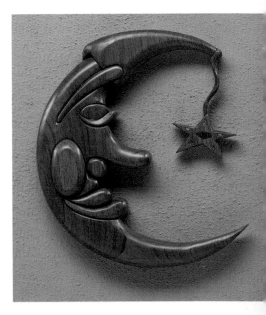

Introduction

The Pattern Companion: Scroll Saw is intended to be both a stimulating resource and an instructional reference for everyone who possesses basic scroll-sawing and woodworking skills. It is for any woodworker looking for inspiration beyond the basic How-To. Rather than elaborating on or repeating basic skill information, it provides a wider range of patterns and useful finishing information.

Expand your vision and have fun. This book will help you learn to think like an artist and experiment with woods, stains, coloring, textures, and various backgrounds or plaque choices that will add to the dramatic effects of your efforts.

Proceed with Safety

Nearly every woodworking task can be performed in more than one way—hand tool versus power tool techniques is one common comparison. The process of using and understanding any power tool will contribute to the success and sense of accomplishment that come with a job well done. Use caution, however, as the materials employed by a craftsperson can be dangerous and potentially lethal. The combination of potentially noxious dust, harmful chemicals and paints, high noise levels, sharp tools, and high quantities of electricity make it imperative that the craftsperson operates in a safe, clean, and well thought-out environment.

The risk of injury should never be underestimated. Use common sense at all times so that each new challenging project proves to be rewarding and satisfying.

Safety Guidelines

- Understand and strictly observe manufacturer's instructions for the safe operation of all tools.
- Always wear a respirator or dust mask while working.
- Wear eye and ear protection when working with power tools.
- Never allow fingers to come near any moving blades or cutters.
- Wear a shop apron and appropriate attire—no jewelry, loose sleeves, ties.
- Feel comfortable when using power tools. Think out your project in its entirety and understand all aspects of it before beginning.
- Always keep your mind on your work. Do not allow your mind to wander or be distracted when using power tools or sharp objects.
- Above all, never work when tired, in a hurry, or not in the mood. Put the project down and come back to it later, in a better frame of mind and with time to spare.

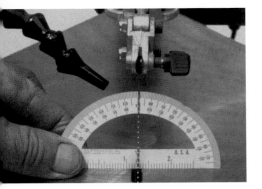

Using a simple protractor is the easiest way to check the squareness of the table to the blade and to adjust table tilt to the desired angle for bevel cutting.

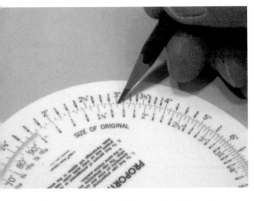

A proportion scale is used to determine optimum sizes when reducing or enlarging patterns on a photocopy machine. Simply align the mark indicating the existing size of the pattern in the book, then turn the scale to the desired finished size and take note of the percentage in the window. Set the copy machine to the percentage designated in the proportion scale's window.

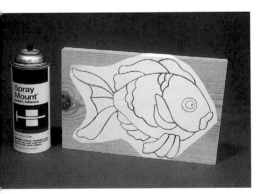

Adhere a photocopy of the pattern to the wood with temporary bond adhesive spray applied to the back of the pattern only.

Prepare the Saw

Make certain to first read and review the owner's manual and observe all of the safety precautions relative to the use of the scroll saw. For most of the projects, it is necessary to make cuts with the saw table set square to the blade. Use a small square or protractor to make and check this adjustment. The factory calibrations on the blade-tilt scales of most scroll saws are difficult to read (especially with bifocals) and most are not accurate. Make certain that the blade is installed with the teeth pointing downward. Tension it correctly, according to the manufacturer's instructions.

Technique Instructions

Unless otherwise specified in individual project instructions, following these steps:

1. Select the wood. Sand and smooth the surface and remove excess dust with a tack cloth.

2. Determine if the pattern will be used as presented or if size adjustments need to be made. Consider also the sizes of selected wood to be used for the project. (A slight size reduction of the pattern may allow for refitting it onto a piece of wood that would otherwise be cast aside.) Use a proportion scale to help determine the exact percentage of reduction or enlargement required before making a photocopy of the pattern. Reduce or enlarge the pattern to any size desired at a copy shop or using an available copy machine, making two photocopies of the pattern—one for cutting and the other to use later to assemble the segments on.

3. Using scissors, cut the excess paper from around one copy of the pattern, leaving about 1/2" beyond the shape of the design. The wood should be slightly larger than the copy. Spray the back of the copy with adhesive spray. Allow to dry about 30 seconds and hand-press the copy to the face surface of the wooden work piece. The work piece is now ready for cutting.

4. Cut out the segments. For most projects, the pattern provides thin cutting lines to follow. Cut either directly on the line or slightly to one side of it. However, take care not to cut too far outside the line as the integrity of the design may be spoiled. Patience and practice are the keys to developing cutting skills. The most difficult types of cuts to make accurately are perfectly straight lines or parallel lines that run close together, a true radius or full circle, and other geometric shapes, such as ovals, triangles and squares. Beginners should use the hold-down and guard.

5. Making quick, sharp, "on-the-spot" turns to cut inside corners and acute angles requires practice and a fairly narrow blade. For projects that have inside segments that must be cut out, simply drill a very small hole through the work piece in an inconspicuous place along the pattern line. Thread the blade through the hole in the work piece, reattach it to the saw and begin cutting.

6. Mark the backs of the segments and remove the paper pattern from the fronts.

Tips

Cut 1/4" plywood and thinner on a slow-speed saw. If a slow-speed saw is not available, add extra stability to the project by using a waste-backer nailed, glued, or affixed with double-sided tape under the work piece. A waste-backer adds "blade resistance," resulting in better cutting control. The waste-backer also minimizes tear-out and splintering on the bottom of the work piece. Previously used plywood or paneling makes an effective and inexpensive waste-backer material.

When securing a waste-backer under the work piece with nails, drive small brads through the waste areas of both pieces while held over a flat piece of metal. The metal will peen the nails on the bottom side. This technique works well with plywood as thin as 1/32"-thick.

The same techniques can be employed when stack-cutting. Stack-cutting is a good production technique as it involves placing two or more layers, one on top of the other, securing them together so they do not slip or shift, and cutting all layers at once.

Small holes are drilled to cut out these concentric circular segments of a fish eye. The hole slots made by the drill can be hidden with wood filler and paint.

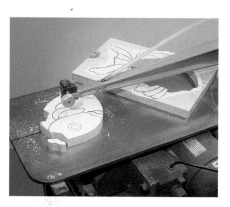

Use a No. 5 ground blade for best results when cutting the segments.

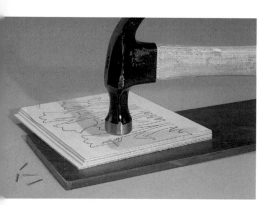

Stack-cutting is cutting two or more layers of materials at the same time. Here, the pieces are tacked together with brads driven through the waste areas while held over a flat piece of metal.

BASIC TOOLS & SUPPLIES

Acrylic paints
Adhesive spray: temporary
    bonding aerosol
Blades
Brads: small
Carving knives
Chisels
Colored dyes: transparent
Colored paints: opaque
Copy paper
Cotton cloth
Craft knife
Craft scissors
Dowels
Drill and drill bits
Emery boards
Files
Flutter wheel: 150 or 180 grit
Finish: natural
Paintbrushes
Paper towels
Pencil
Picture frame hangers: sawtooth
Pliers
Plywood: 1/8"- to 1/4"-thick
    for waste backers
Proportion scale
Rasps
Rotary tool: high-speed with
    various accessories
Sanders: belt or disk with coarse
    abrasives, 36 to 50 or 60 grit;
    drum; orbital
Sandpaper
Scroll sanders
Scroll saw
Sponge brushes
Square or protractor: small
Stains: colored; oil
Tack cloth
Tape: double-sided
Trim router and bits
Waxed paper, freezer paper, or
    plastic wrap
Wood-burning tool
Wood glue (yellow carpenter's
    glue) or instant/super glues

Decorative Scroll Saw

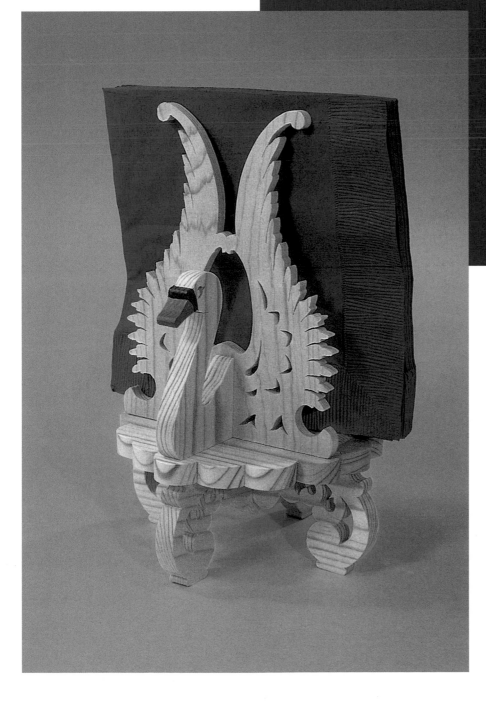

Ornaments are typically small, fun, easy-to-make projects for gifts or personal use. They also have great market potential for those woodworkers wanting to sell their work in shops and at craft fairs. The patterns provided in this first section are all full size and are the creation of Dirk Boelman, America's leading scroll-saw pattern designer. His designs and artwork regularly grace the pages of *Creative Wood Works and Crafts* magazine, as well as the magazine's annual special-edition publication, "Wood Ornaments."

Scrollers are permitted to make any number of projects from this fine selection of ornamental and decorative patterns, as long as they are hand-cut using conventional scroll saws. To obtain the greatest possible use of the patterns, consider enlarging them substantially to create yard art and exterior home decorations, or reduce the same patterns to create interesting miniatures.

Some projects feature decorative "add-ons" such as leather, bright-colored cords, ribbons, beads, feathers, clock and photo inserts, and decorative hardware. Most of these items are readily available at craft and hobby shops, leather-working stores, or by mail order; or use your ingenuity and creativity to substitute!

Solid white acrylic plastic with a blue translucent backer makes a striking ornament. Clear silicon adhesive was used.

Material Choices

Select quality hardwood plywoods when thin stock is specified and where strength is important. Highly detailed fretwork and toys will be more durable if cut from plywood.

All plans and patterns are drawn in U.S. (Imperial) dimensions. Therefore, slight adjustments must be made to the patterns when using materials of metric sizes. (Refer to the Metric Conversion chart on page 187.) This is especially true when you are making three-dimensional projects with halved joints. Baltic birch plywood 6mm in thickness, for example, is close to 1/4" but it is actually slightly thinner.

Use solid hardwoods for making household accessories and all projects that will look better without plywood edges. Consider using plastics, paper, metal, and other materials to obtain visual variety using the same pattern.

Finishes

As a general rule, avoid high-gloss finishes on natural wood and fretwork pieces. On pieces you intend to paint, use acrylics because of their quick-drying quality and easy water cleanup. Consider using the many specialty spray finishes available, including flock, crackle, faux stone, marble, and metallic. Not only is application convenient, but you can easily create dramatic effects. Specialty sprays are available in a variety of finishes

Bright gold aerosol finish gives 1/8" Baltic birch a brilliant metallic look. (See page 00.)

Preparation for an easy-to-achieve patina finish on 1/8" plywood. First the project is coated with a clear sealer followed with a coat or two of water-based bronze or copper liquid metal, as shown here.

A sponge application of the patina solution provides an un-patterned contrast that oxidizes the metallic substrate. This creates a remarkable resemblance to real aged metal. (See the patina-finished projects on pages 17, 50, and 143.)

Ornamental Projects
Decorative Birds

Make bodies from 1/8" thick material.

Make tails and wings from 1/32" thick material.

Suspend your completed birds from a hoop, branch, etc. Carefully determine the balancing point; drill a small hole and thread fish line through it.

Cardinal and Blue Jay

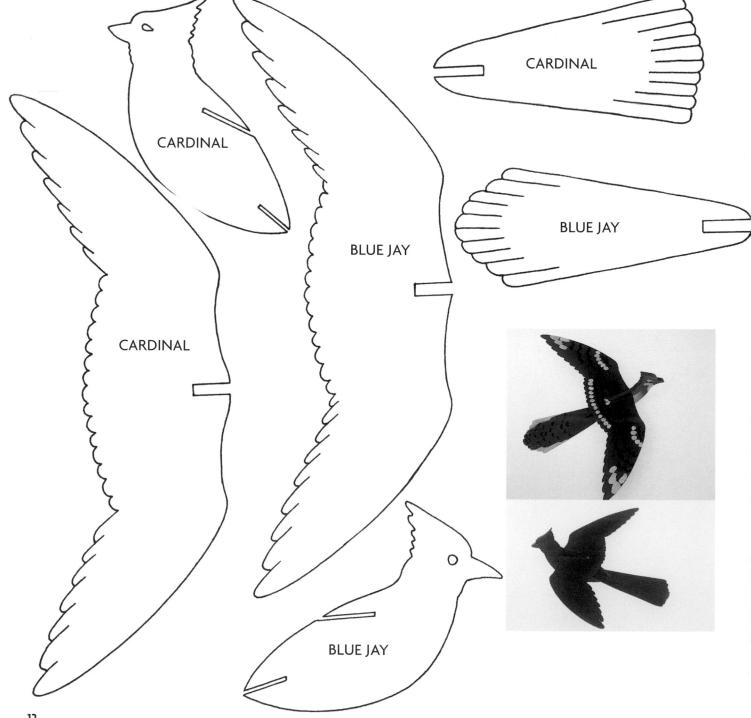

CARDINAL

CARDINAL

CARDINAL

CARDINAL

BLUE JAY

BLUE JAY

BLUE JAY

Dove and Swallow

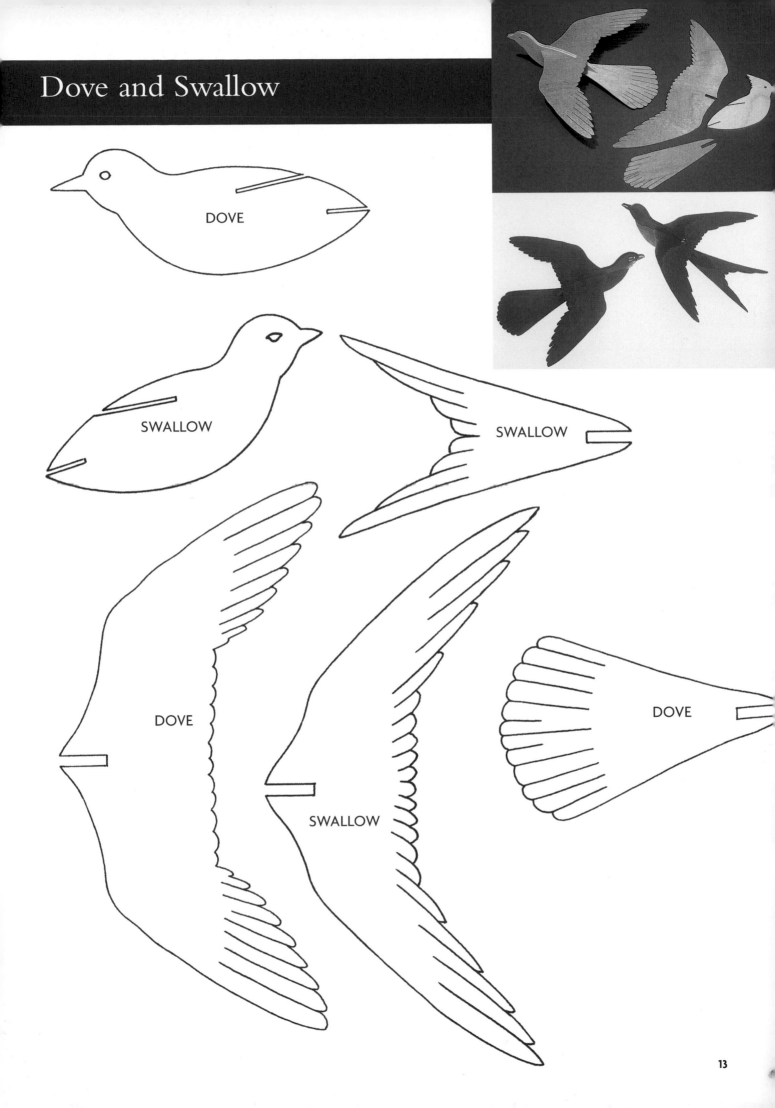

DOVE

SWALLOW

SWALLOW

DOVE

SWALLOW

DOVE

Humming Bird and Robin

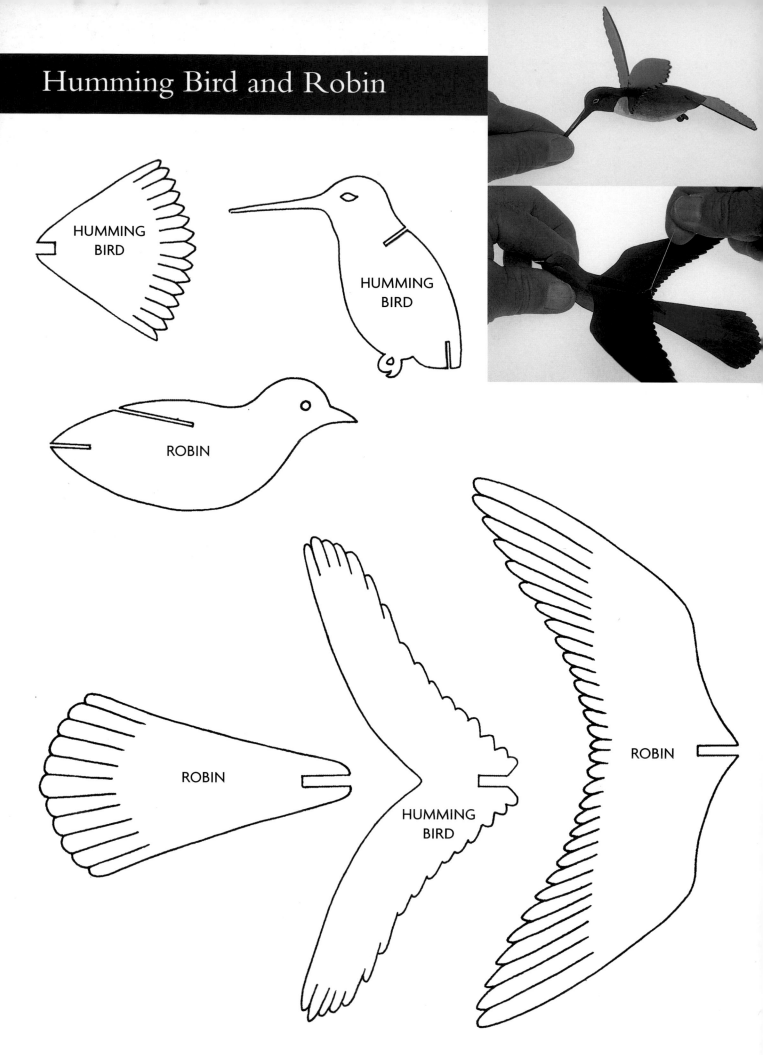

HUMMING
BIRD

HUMMING
BIRD

ROBIN

ROBIN

HUMMING
BIRD

ROBIN

Southwest Designs

Note that variations include using real feathers as well as the scroll-cut wooden ones.

American Eagle

Saw the eagle from a separate piece of material, and overlay it on a circular backer board of contrasting color.

Patina-finished plywood on a solid copper backer.

Animal March

Enlarge the pattern 200 percent on a photocopy machine.

Make the base from 3/4" thick material

Bevel or shape edges as desired. (We chose a 30 degree bevel.)

Join patterns along line A–B.

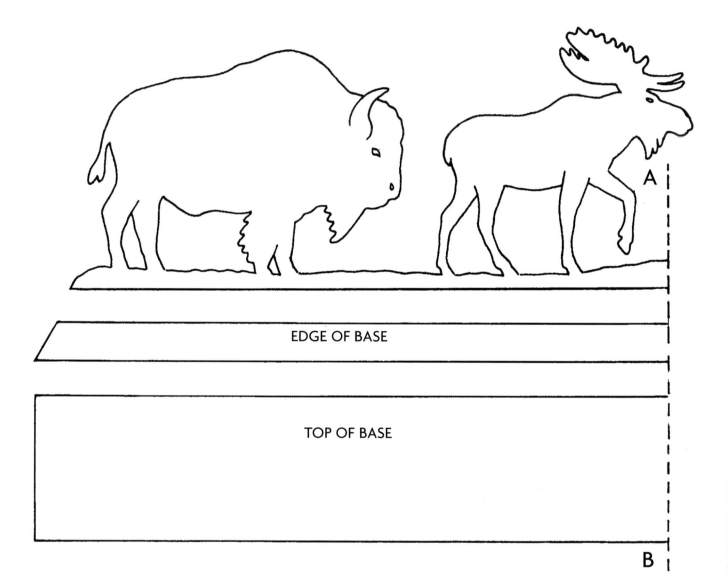

EDGE OF BASE

TOP OF BASE

A

B

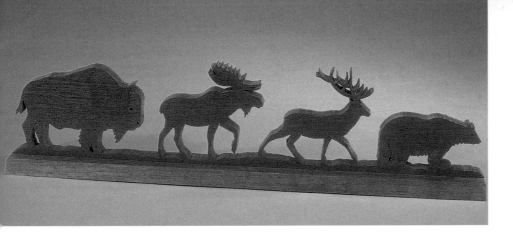

A

B

Butterfly

Make various sizes of butterflies from your favorite colors of wood, or paint and stain as desired. Ideas include: making two at a time and sandwiching them together with thin colored plastic; or, eliminate all of the interior cutouts and just paint the spots on your butterflies.

Feline

Cut from ⅛" thick plywood.

Clown

The Clown works well as a wall hanging.

Toys & Doll Furniture
Victorian Doll Chair

The chair has an upholstered appearance by applying fabric-covered cardboard to the seat and back.

Chair sides: make from 1/4" thick material.

Make 2 sides for each chair.

Back and Seat: make from 1/4" thick material.

HOW TO MAKE THE CUSHIONS:

Make seat and back cushions by cutting a piece of cardboard to the size of the dashed outlines shown on the patterns.

Cut pieces of fabric approx. 1/2" wider and longer than the cardboard.

Wrap the fabric around the cardboard; glue the fabric to back of cardboard.

Glue the cardboard and fabric assembly in place onto chair.

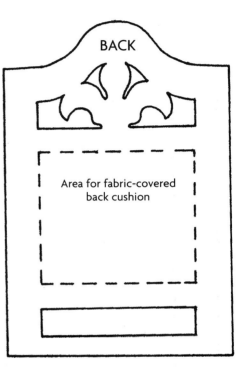

BACK

Area for fabric-covered back cushion

SEAT

Area for fabric-covered seat cushion

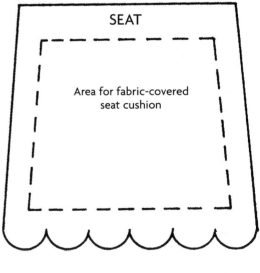

CHAIR SIDES

TOP VIEW OF CHAIR BACK

Bevel edges 5 degrees

23

Victorian Doll Couch

Arm sections: make 2 from 1/4" thick material.

The dashed outlines show where the couch's back, seat, and front apron pieces are glued to the arm sections.

Back for couch: make from 1/4" thick material. Bevel the ends at 11°.

Seat for couch: make from 1/4" thick material.

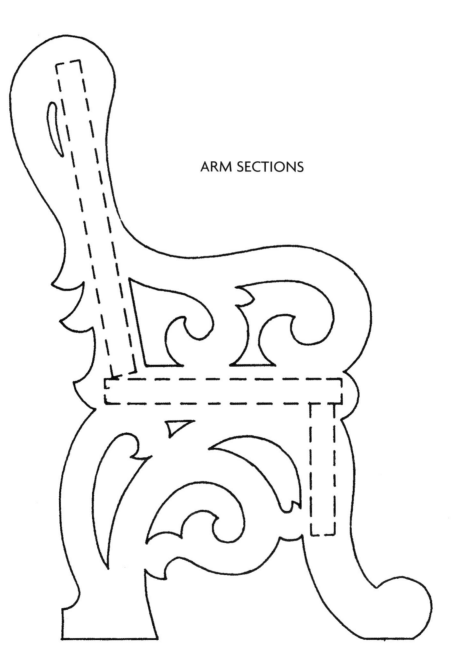

ARM SECTIONS

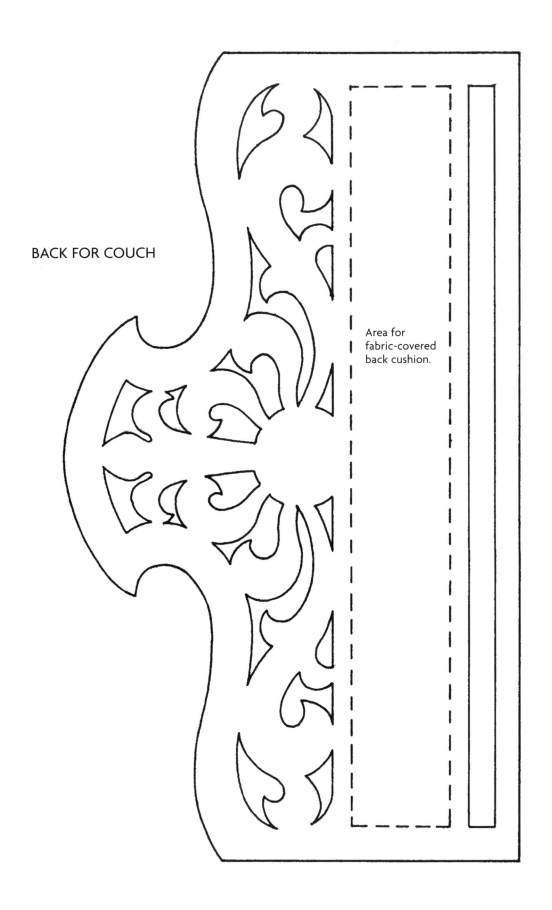

BACK FOR COUCH

Area for fabric-covered back cushion.

SEAT FOR COUCH

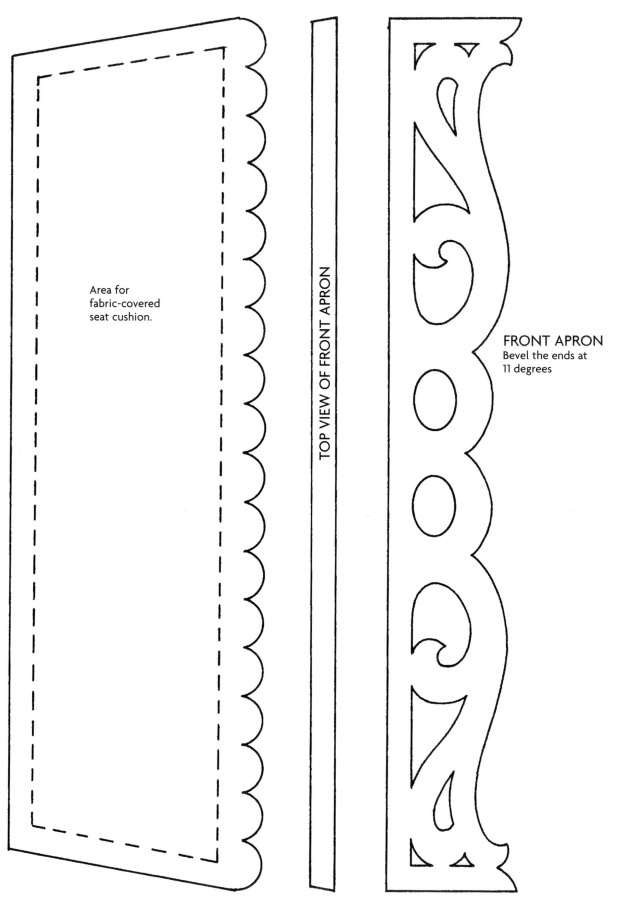

Area for
fabric-covered
seat cushion.

TOP VIEW OF FRONT APRON

FRONT APRON
Bevel the ends at
11 degrees

Victorian Doll Table

Make from 1/4" thick material.
Tabletop: make 2 copies of the pattern and join them along centerline.
Table legs: join along the halved–joint..

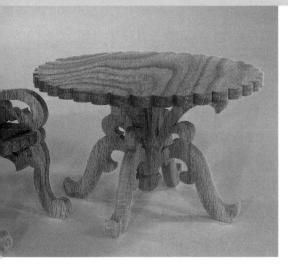

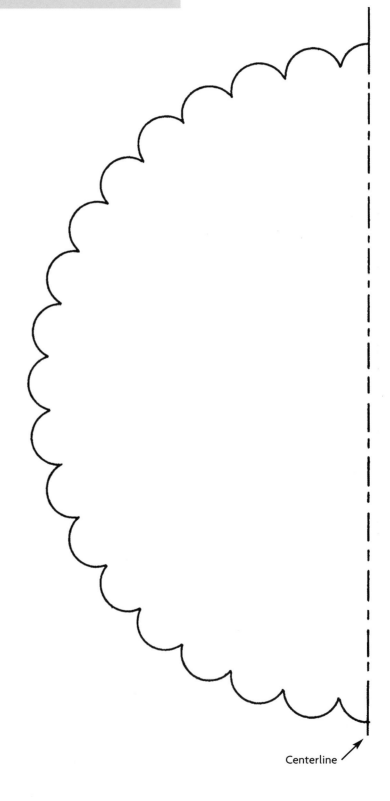

Centerline

Adjust the width of the joint to fit.

Jumping Jack Santa and His Helpers

Traditional "Jumping Jack" figures are quick and easy to make from 1/4" thick material.

HOW TO MAKE THE SANTA & HELPERS "JUMPING JACK" TOYS

Adhere the patterns to the wood with spray glue.

Saw only on the outlines of the patterns.

Drill 1/16" diameter holes at the dots on the patterns of the arms and legs.

Drill 1/8" diameter holes at the +'s on the patterns

Note: Before assembly, paint all the parts as desired, then redrill holes to allow arms and legs to move freely.

Also before assembly, loop strings through the arms and legs as shown in the drawing below right. The strings need to be long enough to extend a few inches below the feet when assembled.

After looping the strings, attach the arms and legs to the body with the brass fasteners.

Tie the strings together as shown in the drawing above right. Make a knot near the middle of the back to join the arm strings; then gather and knot all of the strings approx. 1" below the leg pivots; add a final knot 2" below the feet.

Trim off the strings about 1" below the knot. (If desired, a colorful bead can be added above the knot.)

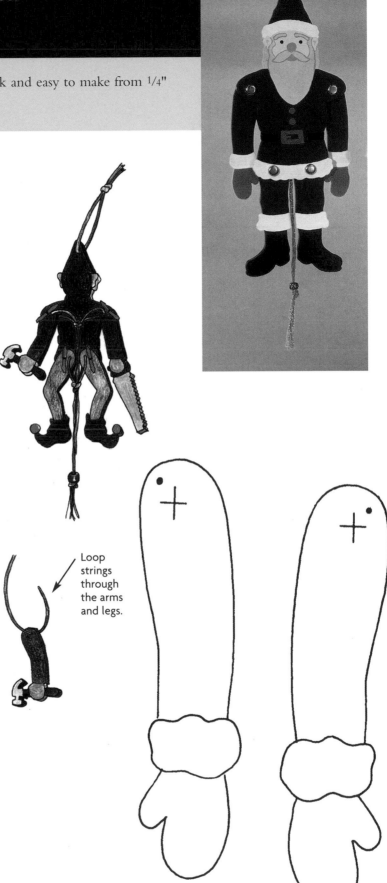

Loop strings through the arms and legs.

Pete the Painter

Refer to page 29 for how to make
the Jumping Jack toys.

Santa's Helpers' arms and legs are
interchangeable.

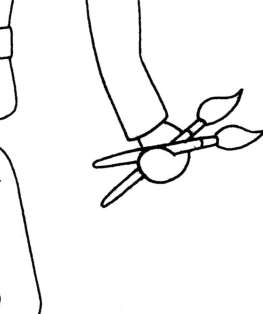

Bob the Builder

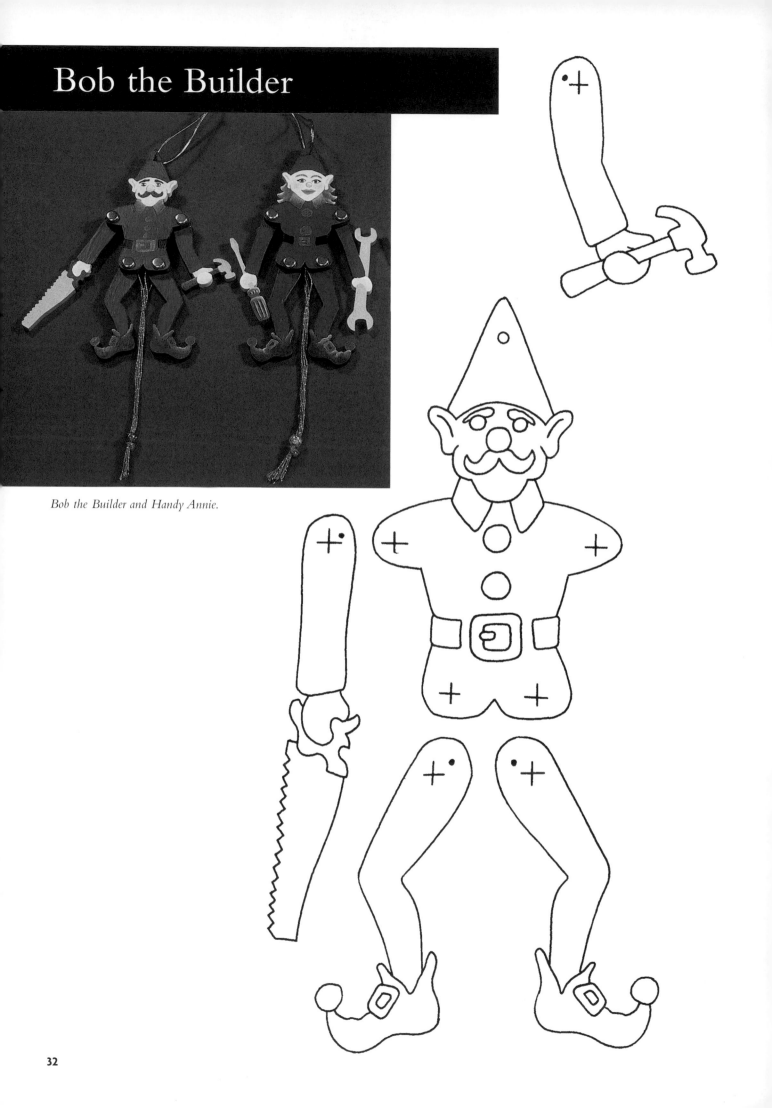

Bob the Builder and Handy Annie.

Handy Annie

Tom the Tailor

To hang your completed project, drill a 1/8" diameter hole at the location shown on the hat, and hang with string or ribbon.

Arms and legs attach to the body with brass fasteners.

Holiday & Religious
Hanging Ornaments

Ornaments can be made from a variety of materials, but most common is plywood 1/32" to 1/4" thick.

Design Tip

Hang your completed ornaments with festive-colored ribbons, cords, or strings, and decorate them with beads, bells, and other holiday trim.

3-D Ornaments

3-D Ornaments are designed to be made from 1/8" to 1/4" thick material. They use a half-joint to fasten sections together. Since the actual thickness of materials will vary, you may need to adjust the width of the joint on the patterns.

Lay your material on edge over the slotted areas and trace their outline on the pattern. Saw slightly to the inside edges of your newly drawn pattern lines; sand or file to fit.

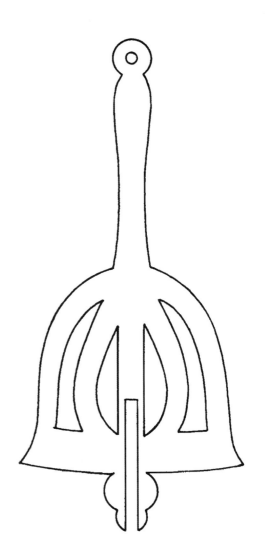

Design Tip

Ornaments can be hung with
traditional wire ornament hangers,
or use festive-colored ribbons,
string, or cord.

Christmas Tree

ake two from 1/4" thick material.

ote: Cut the second piece with the half-joint at the top.

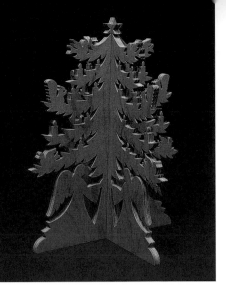

Reindeer

Make reindeer from 1/4" thick material.

Make 1

Make 2

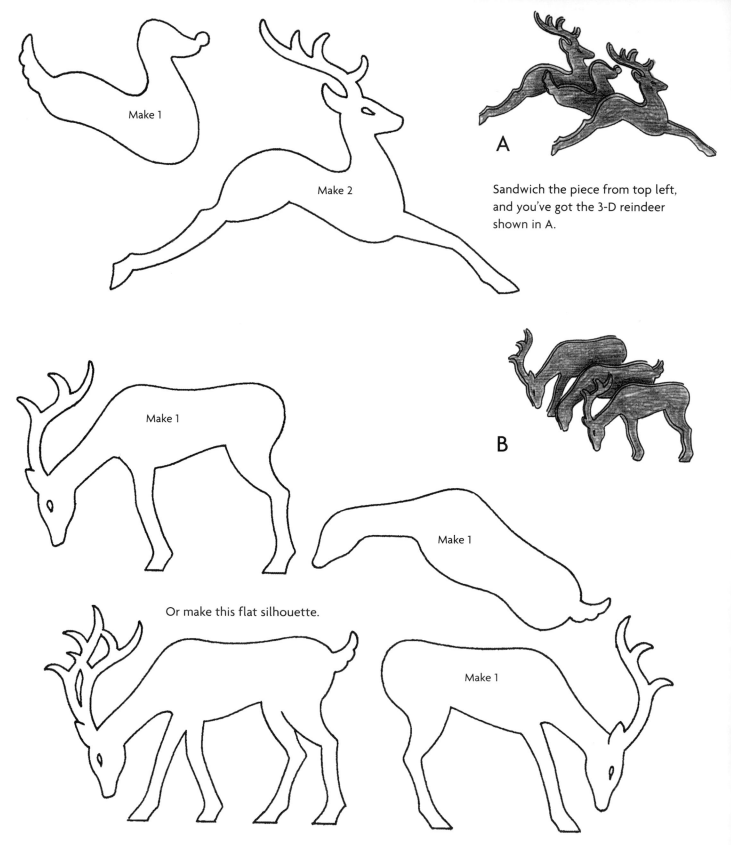

A

Sandwich the piece from top left, and you've got the 3-D reindeer shown in A.

B

Make 1

Make 1

Or make this flat silhouette.

Make 1

Make 1

Make 1

Make 1

Make 1

C

← Or just make this silhouette from one piece of 1/4" thick material.

Nativity Ornaments

This looks great in natural wood tones or can be stained or painted as desired. Acrylic plastic also works well.

Above: 1/8" Baltic Birch with sprayed-on metallic finish.

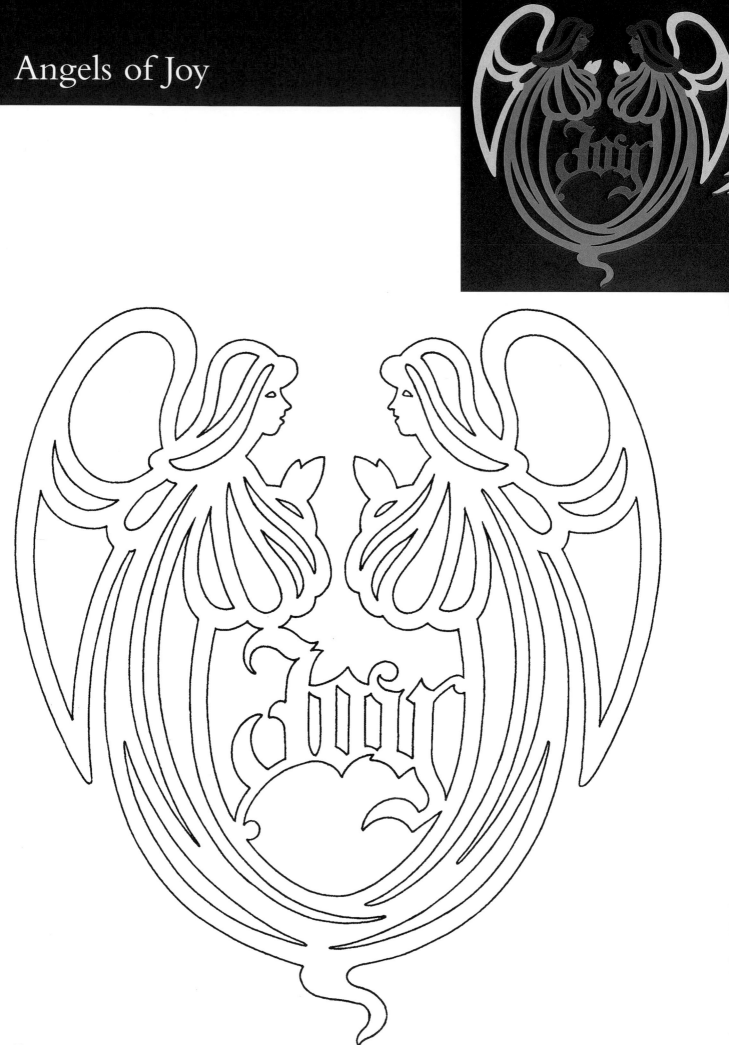

Musical Angel

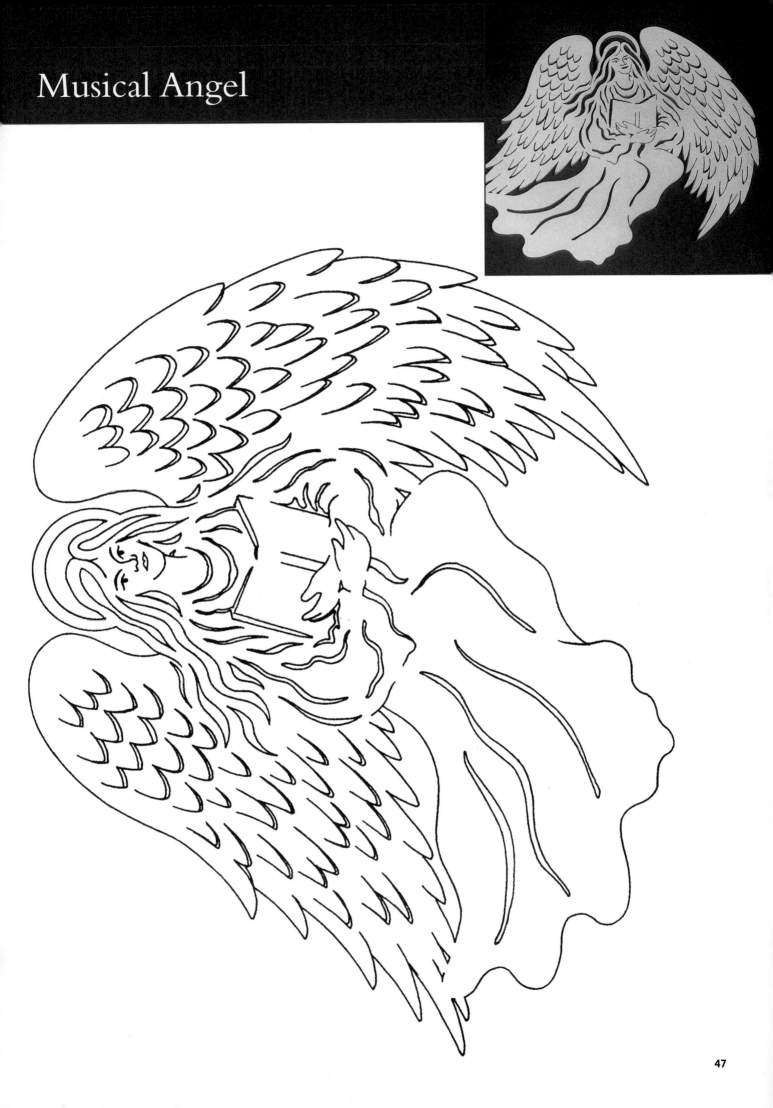

Majestic Cross

Enlarge these cross patterns 130% on a photocopy machine

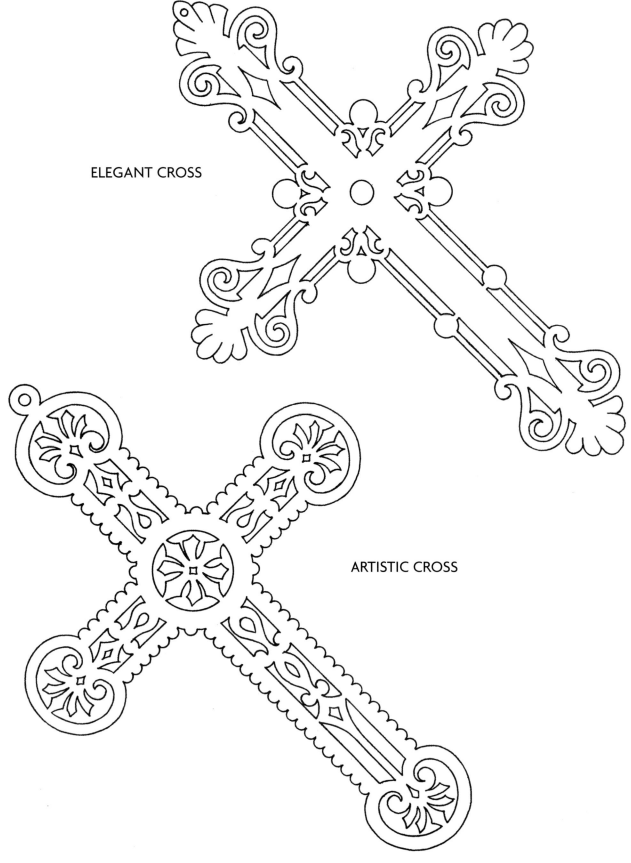

ELEGANT CROSS

ARTISTIC CROSS

Menorah

Make from ⅛" plywood.

This has a patina finish to look like metal.

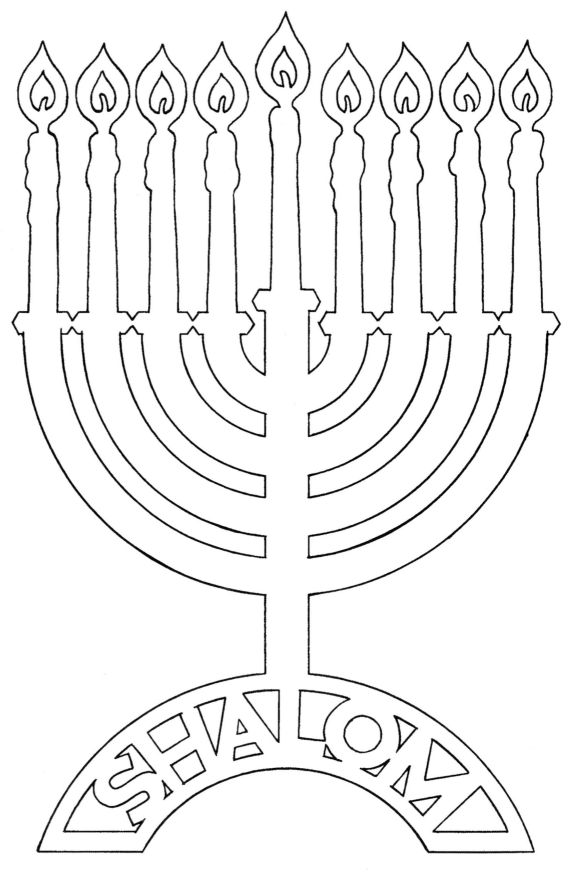

Star of David

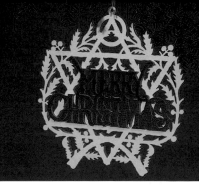

Holiday greetings (next page) can be overlaid on the Star of David.

Holiday Greetings

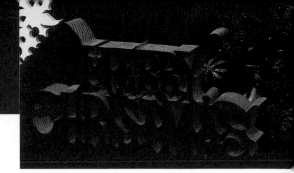

Same lettering pattern cut from ³/4" stock makes a table decoration.

Clocks
Thompson Table Clock

Make from 1/4" thick material.

The Thompson table clock is designed to hold a 2" diameter clock insert. (Modify the size of the mounting hole as needed to fit your insert.)

$1\frac{13}{16}$

$1\frac{3}{8}$

Location of legs

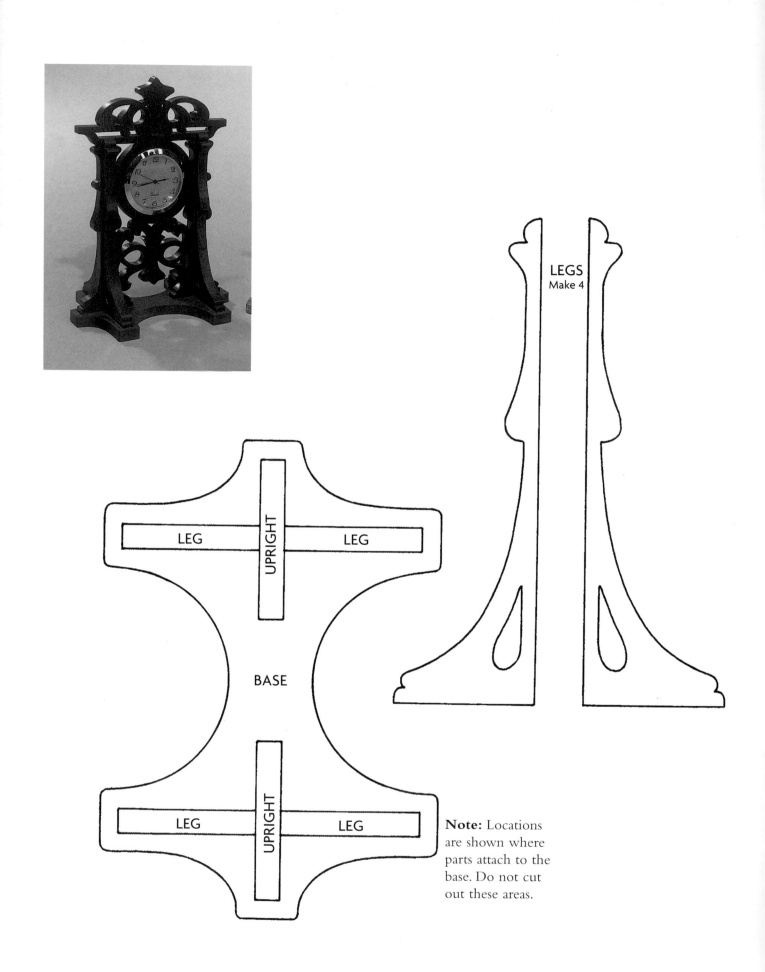

LEGS
Make 4

LEG

UPRIGHT

LEG

BASE

LEG

UPRIGHT

LEG

Note: Locations are shown where parts attach to the base. Do not cut out these areas.

Little Dutch Windmill Clock

Make the building from 3/4" thick material.

It is designed to hold a 1 7/16" diameter clock insert that requires a 1 3/8" diameter mounting hole.

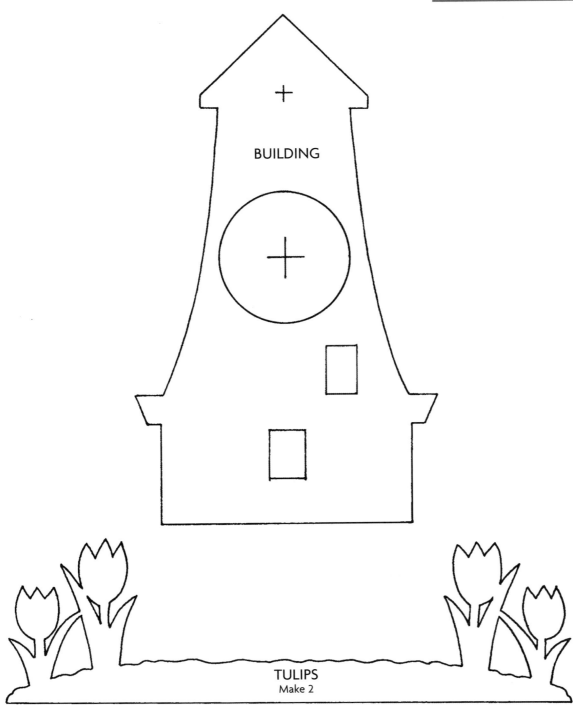

BUILDING

TULIPS
Make 2

BLADES

Drill a small hole in the center to attach to the building with a small nail or brad.

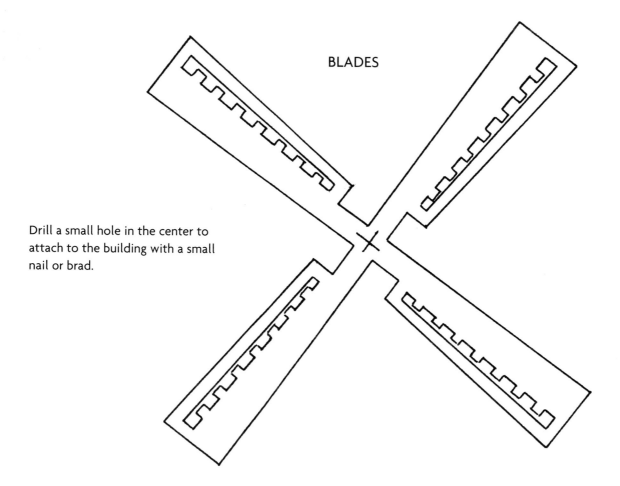

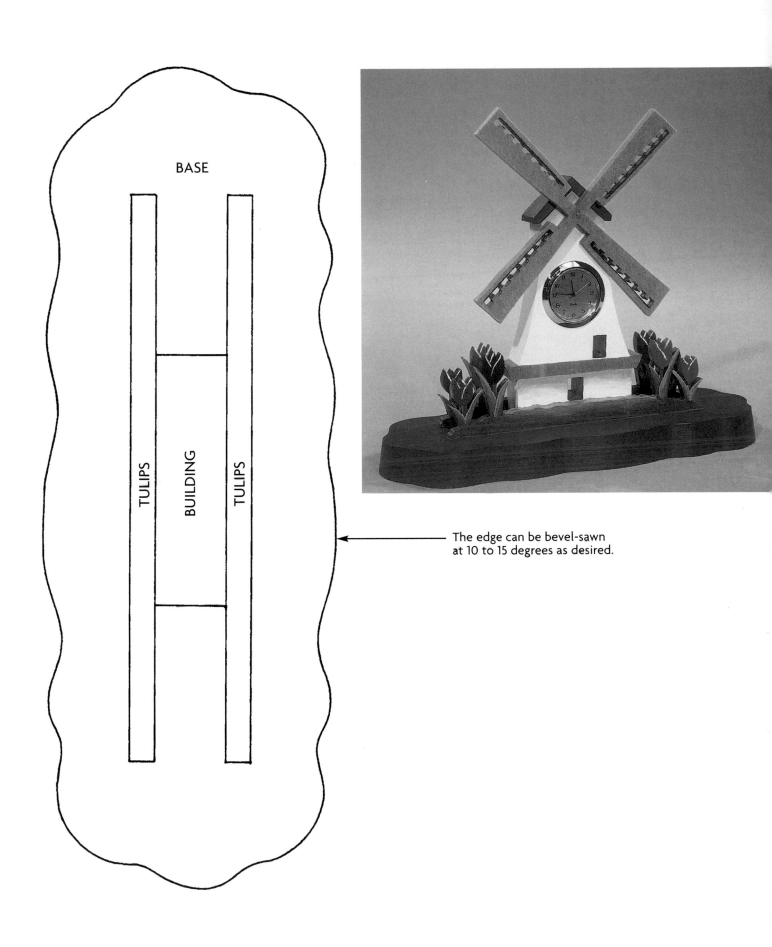

BASE

TULIPS

BUILDING

TULIPS

The edge can be bevel-sawn
at 10 to 15 degrees as desired.

Miniature Kitchen Clock

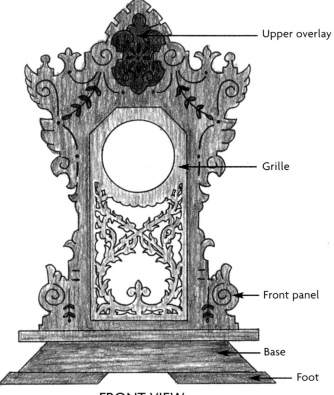

Upper overlay

Grille

Front panel

Base

Foot

FRONT VIEW

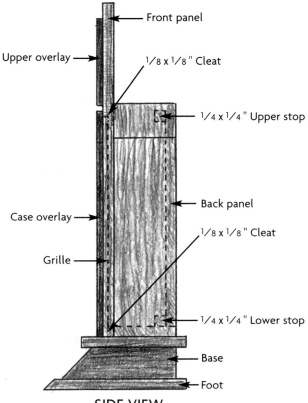

Front panel

Upper overlay

$1/8 \times 1/8$ " Cleat

$1/4 \times 1/4$ " Upper stop

Back panel

Case overlay

$1/8 \times 1/8$ " Cleat

Grille

$1/4 \times 1/4$ " Lower stop

Base

Foot

SIDE VIEW

FRONT PANEL

Make from
1/4" thick
material.

OVERLAY

Make from 1/8" thick
material.

CASE OVERLAY

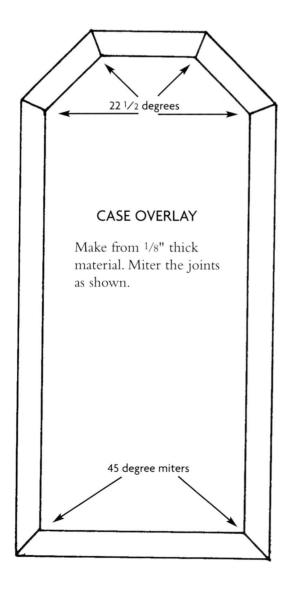

22 1/2 degrees

Make from 1/8" thick
material. Miter the joints
as shown.

45 degree miters

Make from 1/8" thick material.
The grille of this kitchen clock is
designed to hold a 17/16" diameter
clock insert that requires a 13/8"
diameter mounting hole.

GRILLE

CLOCK CASE

Make from six pieces
of 1/4" thick material

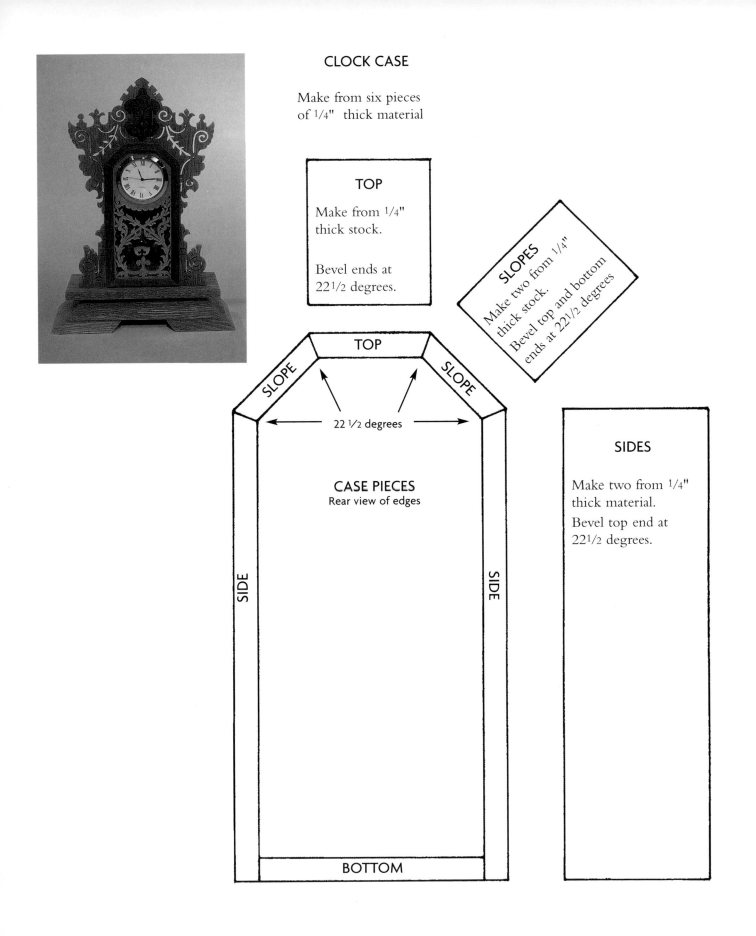

TOP

Make from 1/4"
thick stock.

Bevel ends at
22½ degrees.

SLOPES

Make two from 1/4"
thick stock.

Bevel top and bottom
ends at 22½ degrees

TOP

SLOPE

SLOPE

22 ½ degrees

CASE PIECES
Rear view of edges

SIDE

SIDE

BOTTOM

SIDES

Make two from 1/4"
thick material.

Bevel top end at
22½ degrees.

Make the back panel so that it can be removed for access to the movement. A knob can be fastened to the back if desired.

This clock is designed to utilize a miniature pendulum drive unit, similar to the illustration at right. Follow manufacturer's instructions to install. Attach to the back panel, centered on the location indicated on the pattern. Trim the pendulum rod to the desired length.

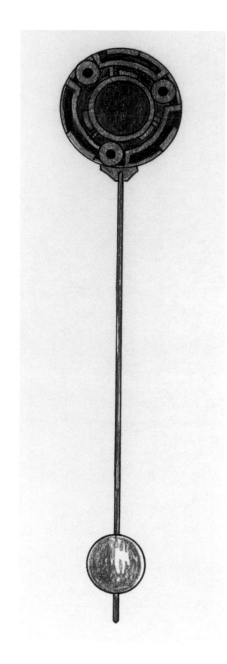

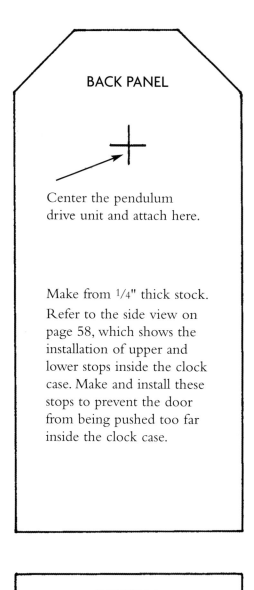

BACK PANEL

Center the pendulum drive unit and attach here.

Make from 1/4" thick stock. Refer to the side view on page 58, which shows the installation of upper and lower stops inside the clock case. Make and install these stops to prevent the door from being pushed too far inside the clock case.

BOTTOM

Make from 1/4" thick stock.

TOP OF BASE

Make from 1/4" thick stock.

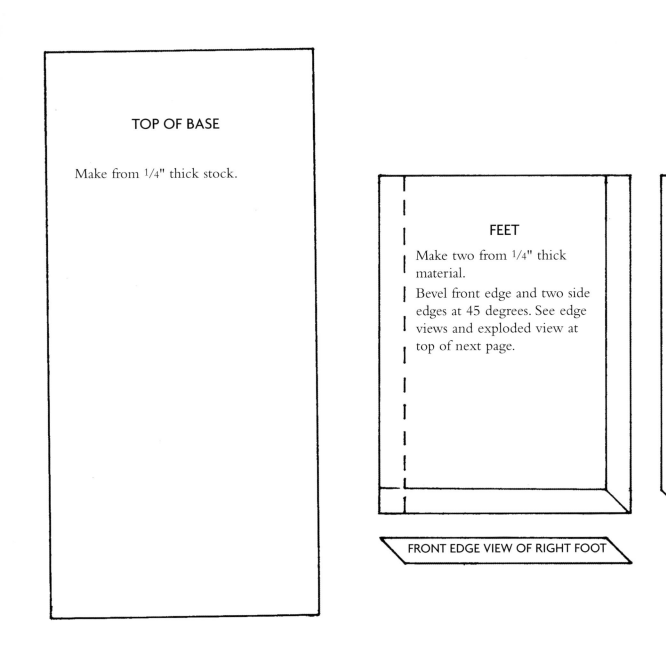

FEET

Make two from 1/4" thick material.

Bevel front edge and two side edges at 45 degrees. See edge views and exploded view at top of next page.

FRONT EDGE VIEW OF RIGHT FOOT

SIDE VIEW OF EDGE OF RIGHT FOOT

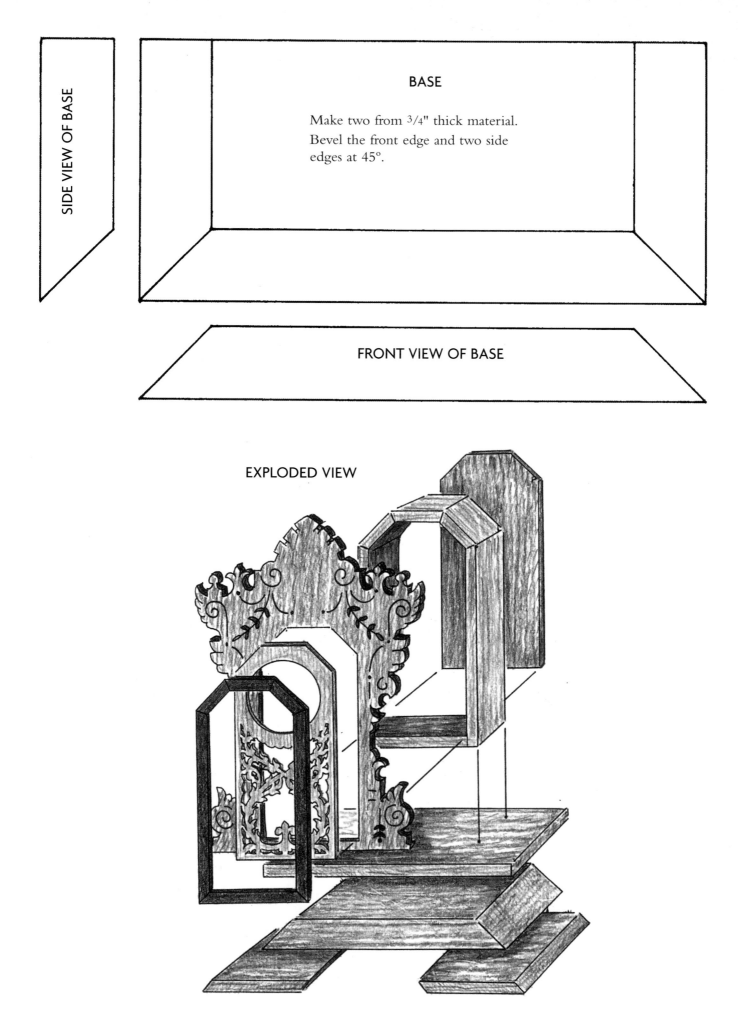

SIDE VIEW OF BASE

BASE

Make two from 3/4" thick material.
Bevel the front edge and two side
edges at 45°.

FRONT VIEW OF BASE

EXPLODED VIEW

Make from 1/2" thick material.

UPRIGHT
Make 2

Bore 9/64" diameter holes for two No. 6 x 1" screws to attach uprights to ends of the shelf.

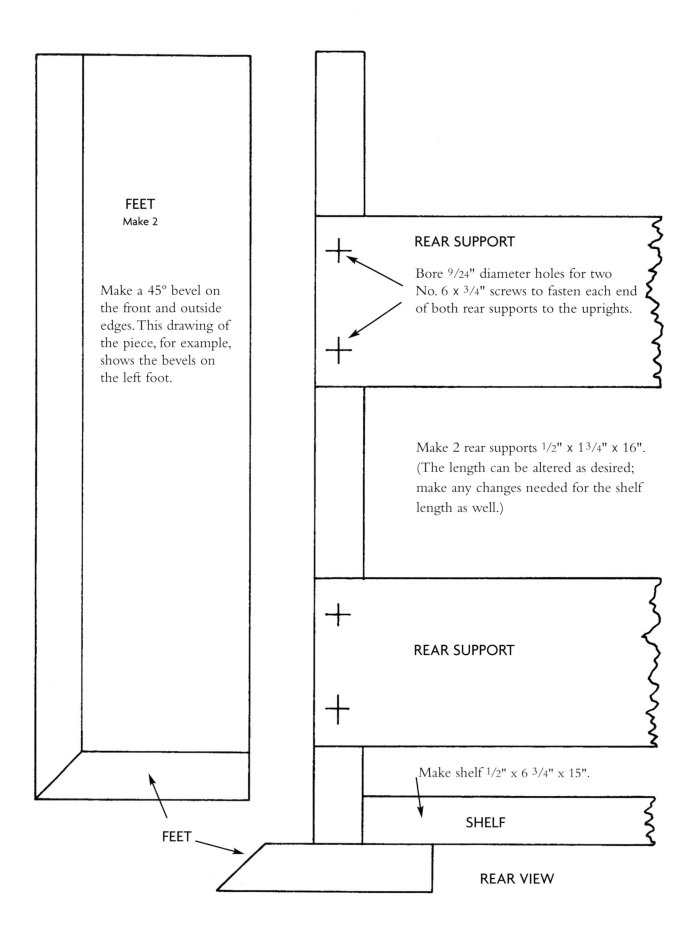

FEET
Make 2

Make a 45° bevel on the front and outside edges. This drawing of the piece, for example, shows the bevels on the left foot.

REAR SUPPORT

Bore $9/24$" diameter holes for two No. 6 x $3/4$" screws to fasten each end of both rear supports to the uprights.

Make 2 rear supports $1/2$" x $1 3/4$" x 16". (The length can be altered as desired; make any changes needed for the shelf length as well.)

REAR SUPPORT

Make shelf $1/2$" x 6 $3/4$" x 15".

SHELF

FEET

REAR VIEW

Scissors Holder

Make from 1/4" thick material.
Join the pattern sections along line (A–B).

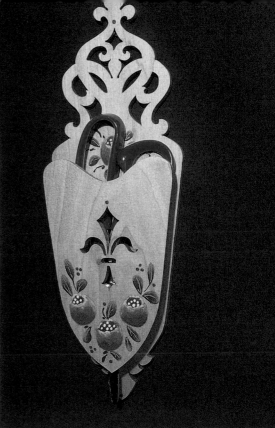

A — — — — — — — — — — — — — — — — B

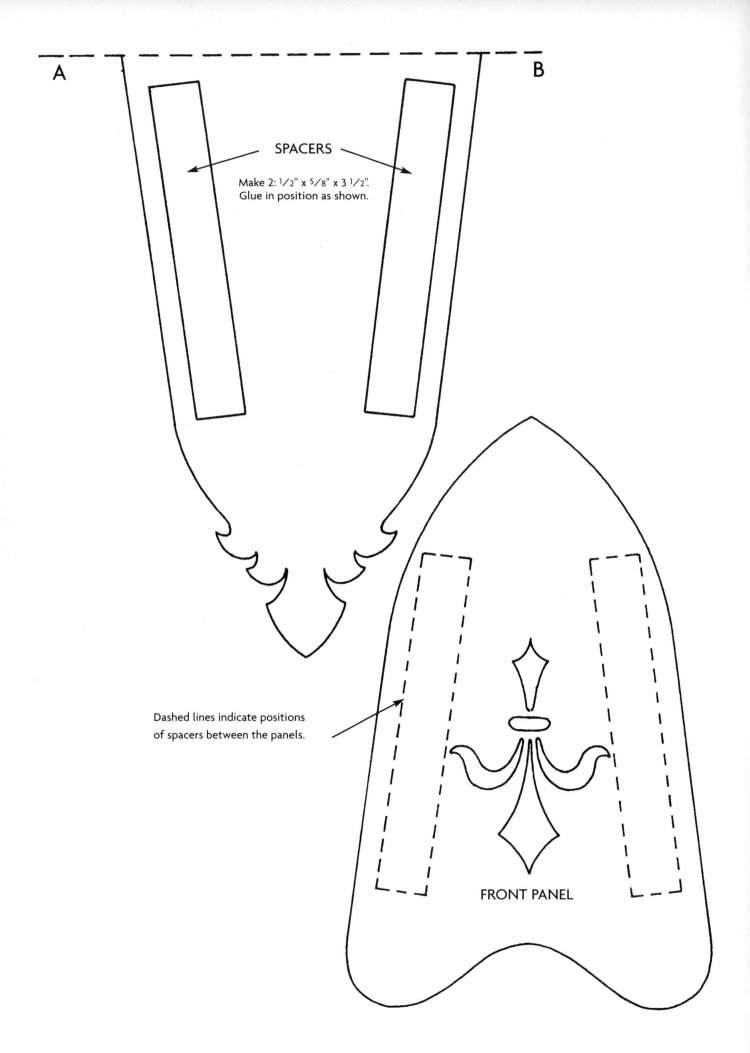

A

B

SPACERS

Make 2: $1/2" \times 5/8" \times 3 1/2"$.
Glue in position as shown.

Dashed lines indicate positions
of spacers between the panels.

FRONT PANEL

Plant Hanger

Enlarge the pattern 200% on a photocopy machine.

Make from 3/4" thick material. Adjust widths of joint areas as needed.

Predrill holes for screws to attach the base to uprights.

When you are ready to assemble all of the pieces, attach the base with glue and wood screws.

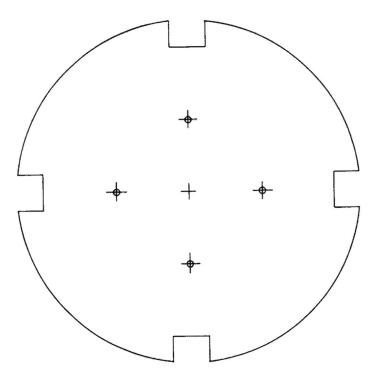

BOTTOM PANEL

Adjust width of joint area, as needed, to match the actual thickness of the material you will be using.

Lay your material on edge directly on the pattern, and trace the outline; saw slightly to the inside edge of your newly drawn pattern lines; sand or file to fit.

JOINT AREA

As with the pattern at left, adjust the joint area to match the actual thickness of the material you will be using.

Lay your material on edge directly on the pattern, and trace the outline; saw slightly to the inside edge of your newly drawn pattern lines; sand or file to fit.

JOINT
AREA

Victorian Wall Shelf

Make from 1/4" thick material.

SHELF SUPPORT
BRACKET

SHELF

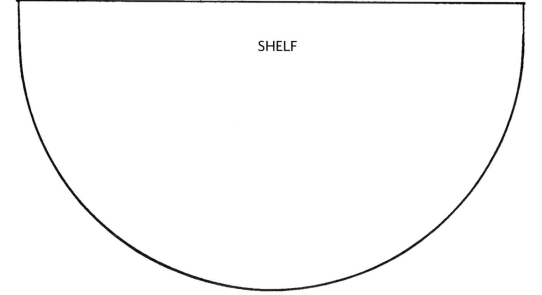

Swan Napkin Holder

Make Wings and Spacer from 1/4" thick material.
Make Heads, Legs and Base from 1/2" thick material.

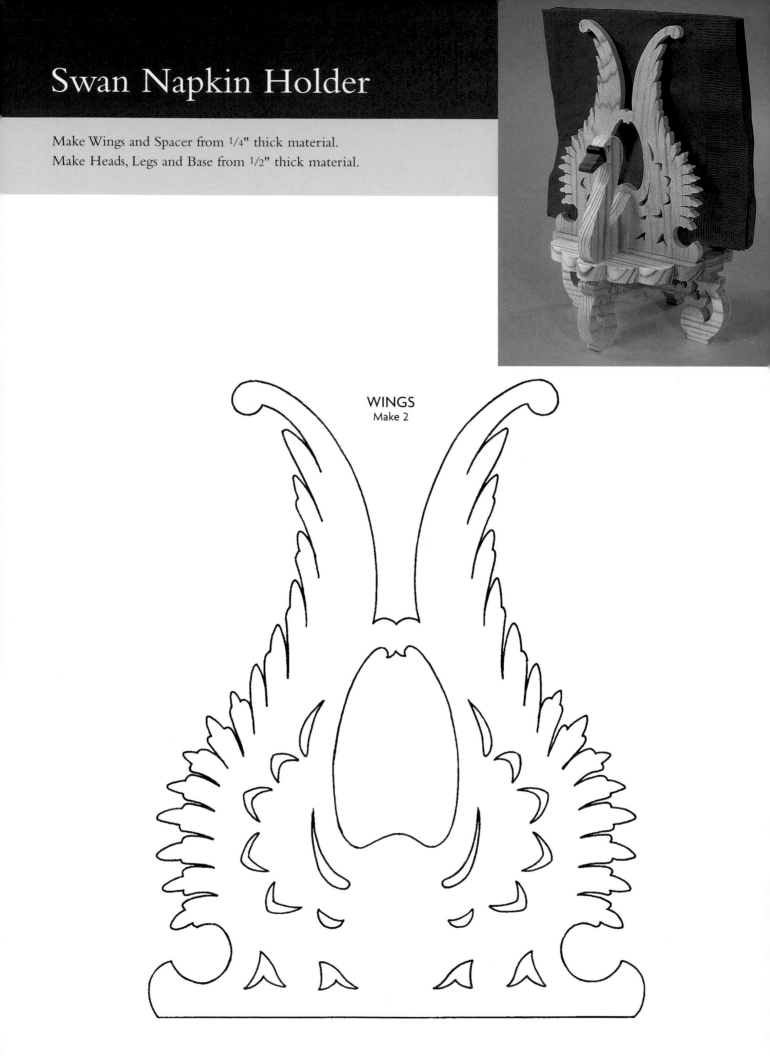

WINGS
Make 2

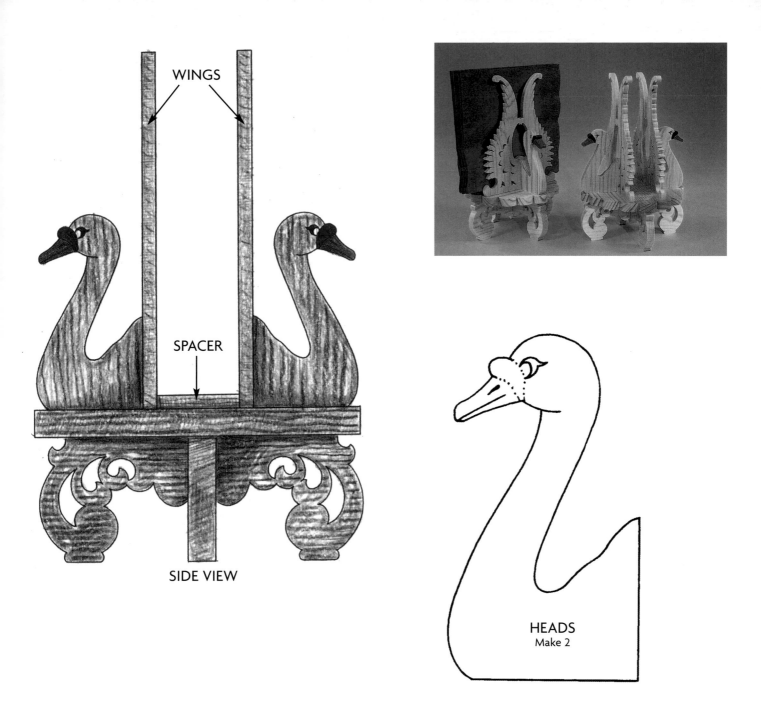

WINGS

SPACER

SIDE VIEW

HEADS
Make 2

SPACER

Since thicknesses of most materials vary, adjust the width of the half-joint to match the material you are using.

Lay your material on edge directly on the pattern, and trace the outline; saw slightly to the inside edge of your newly drawn pattern lines; sand or file to fit.

Half-joint

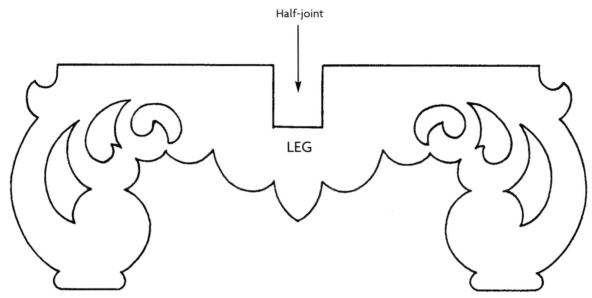

LEG

LEG

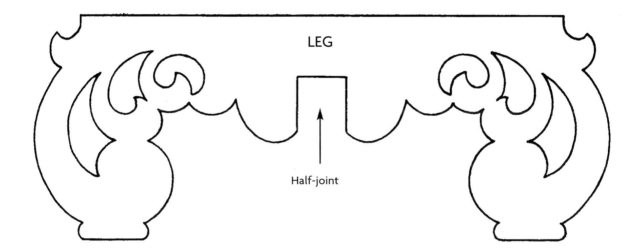

Half-joint

BASE

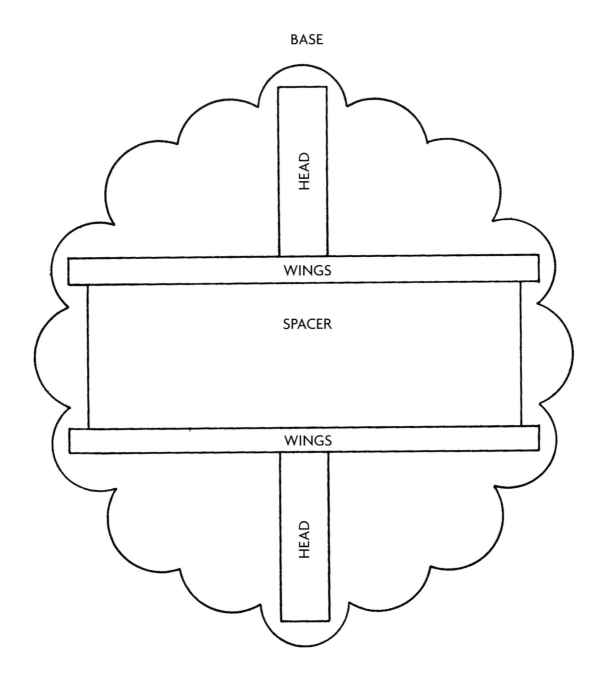

Locations are shown for pieces that attach to top of the base

Signage
House Sign

Make from 1/4" thick material.

Make 2 copies of the pattern on these pages and join the dotted lines together to make the full-size pattern to produce the ornamental background for the sign. (See illustration on the facing page.)

Note: You may want to enlarge the patterns to accommodate long names. You can also reduce or enlarge the alphabet on page 80 to fit.

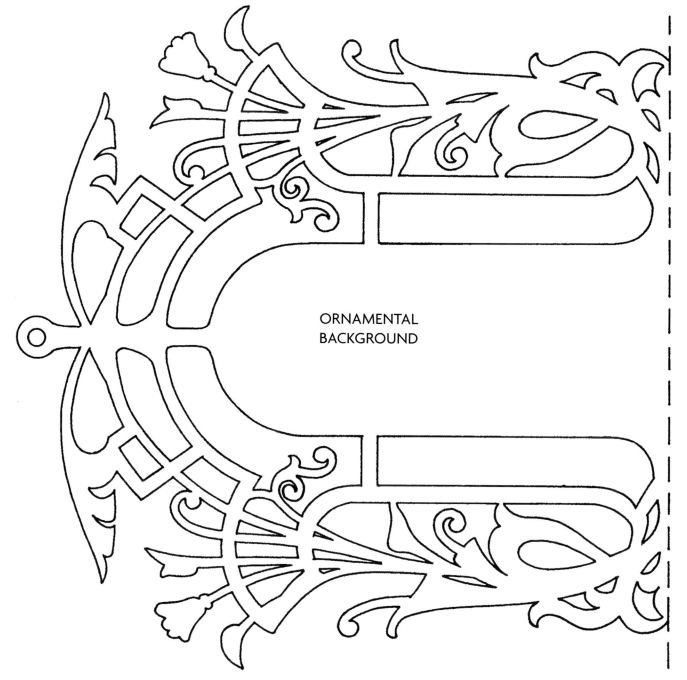

ORNAMENTAL
BACKGROUND

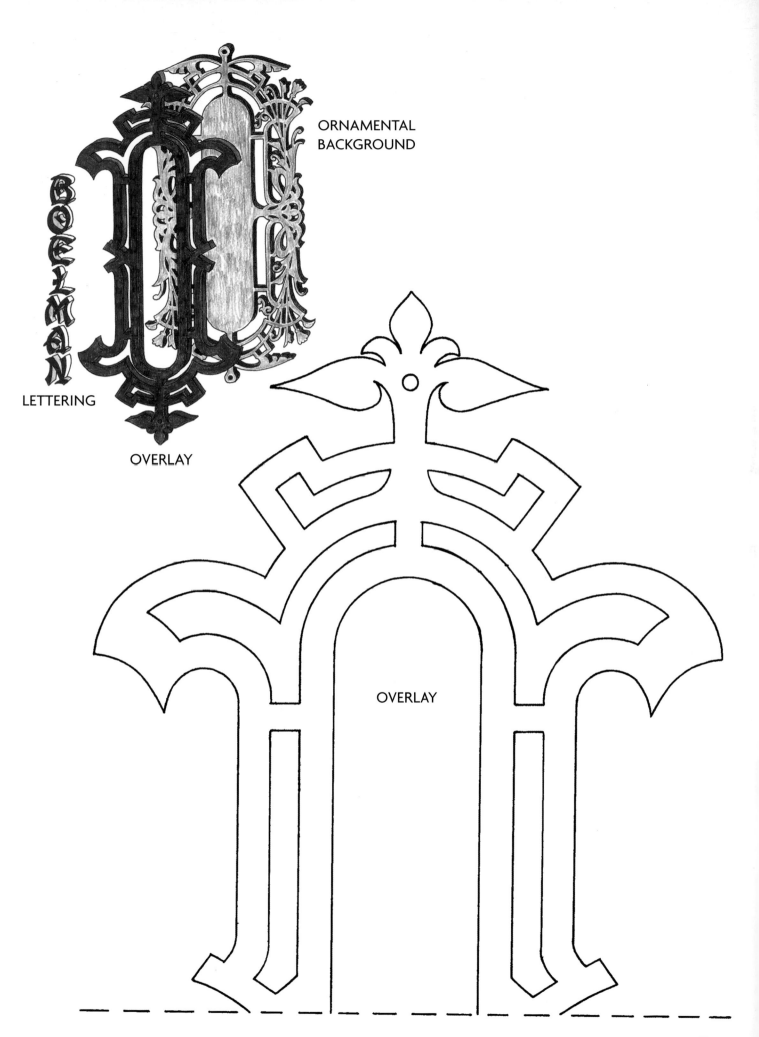

ORNAMENTAL
BACKGROUND

LETTERING

OVERLAY

OVERLAY

Anniversary Gift

Make from 3/4" thick material.

This project is designed to hold a 2" diameter photo frame insert requiring a 1 13/16" diameter mounting hole. Carefully saw on the outermost line or bore with a 1⁶" Forstner bit and enlarge the opening to the outermost line with a drum sander.

Use the contractions below and the numbers opposite to modify the pattern as needed: 1st, 22nd, 25th, 33rd, 40th, or whatever.

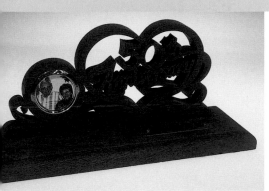

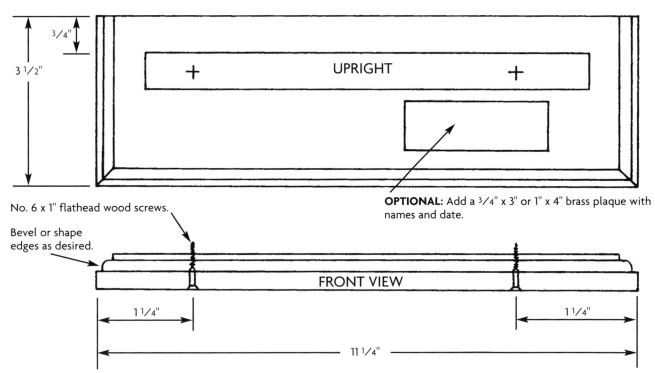

TOP VIEW OF BASE
Shown half size

3/4"

3 1/2"

+   UPRIGHT   +

OPTIONAL: Add a 3/4" x 3" or 1" x 4" brass plaque with names and date.

No. 6 x 1" flathead wood screws.

Bevel or shape edges as desired.

FRONT VIEW

1 1/4"

1 1/4"

11 1/4"

Tying the Knot

A gift to make for newlyweds or wedding anniversaries. Use the following patterns to create names, dates, and decorative elements for the project. Then follow the instructions to make a backer board on which to mount the parts.

DETERMINING THE SIZE OF THE BACKER BOARD

Get a large sheet of paper, approximately 17" x 22". (Or tape smaller sheets together as needed.)

On the paper, draw a vertical line (A–A) down the center. Also draw a horizontal line (B–B) to create the center point on the paper.

Place a compass at the center point and draw a 7 1/8" diameter circle, indicated as (1) on the following page, with a 3 9/16" radius. This is the mounting area for the large decorative circle.

Extend the compass 1" to draw another circle (2). Use this circle as your guide to place the names above the circles, and dates below it, as shown in the illustration on the following page.

Short names like "Dirk & Karen" will fit on one line, but you will need additional circles/lines for longer names such as "Bartholomew and Elizabeth," or to include last names. Extend the compass an additional 1 1/4" for each line, as indicated by circles (3) and (4).

After placing the names and dates in proper locations (centers on the line A–A), determine placements for the corner brackets: Measure the widest portion of your project (e.g., Bartholomew); add a minimum 1/8" beyond each end, and mark to produce two vertical lines (C–C).

From the top edge of the topmost line of letters, add 3/4" and draw a horizontal line (D–D).

Measure down 4 1/4" below circle (1); draw horizontal line (E–E).

Place the large heart 3/8" above line (E–E), and position the four brackets in the corners produced by the lines (C–C, D–D, E–E).

Finally, add a line 1/4" beyond the lines (C–C, D–D, E–E) to define the size of the backer board. (This 1/4" space fits inside rabbet of lip of the frame.)

At this point, observe completed layout and make adjustments as desired. Measure and cut the backer board from 1/4" thick material.

PLANNING THE FRAME

To determine the quantity of material you need for your frame: Measure the width and length of your backer board; add 2" to each dimension, and then double that number. For example: Assume your backer board is 10" x 14 1/2" as shown below. Add 2" to each dimension, making them 12" and 16 1/2". Double these numbers, which equals 24" and 33". Just add these together for a total of 57" of framing material needed.

BACKER BOARD

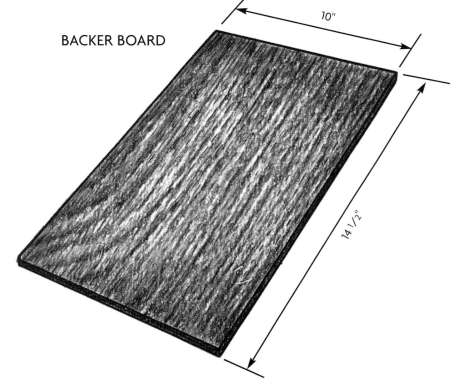

10"

14 1/2"

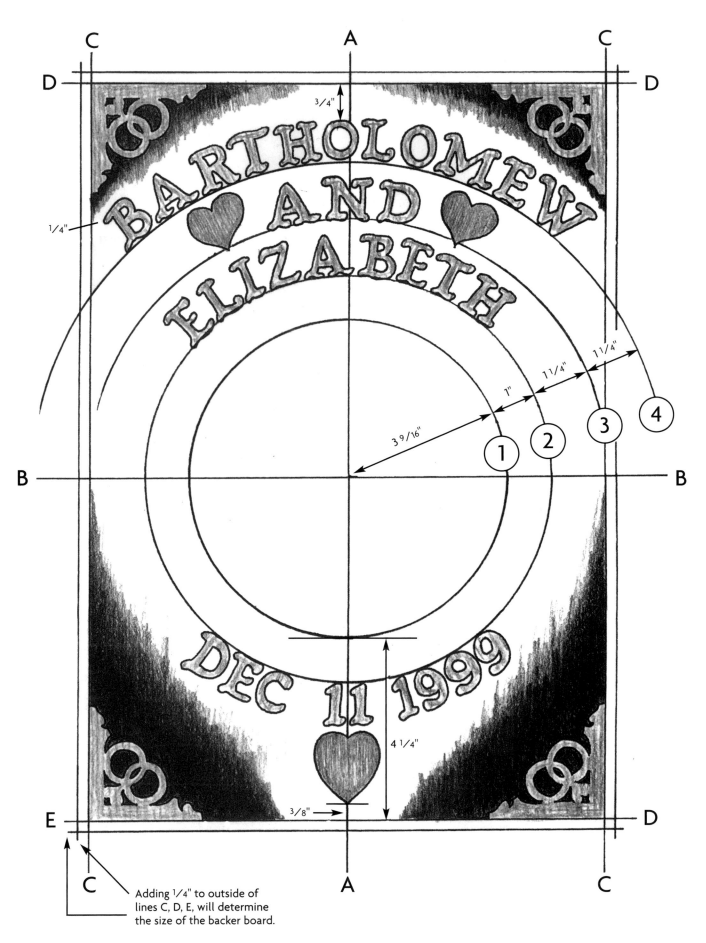

Adding 1/4" to outside of
lines C, D, E, will determine
the size of the backer board.

MAKING THE FRAME . . .

The frame is made from
5/8" x 1 1/8" material. On the bottom edge, use a router and bit to create a rabbet or lip 1/4" wide by 1/4" deep. Use a round-over bit to shape the top edge as shown to the right.

CUTTING FRAME PIECES TO SIZE

Once again, refer to the dimensions of your backer board. Add 1 3/4" to both dimensions. (For example, using our backer board illustrated on facing page, which is 10" x 14 1/2", 10" + 1 3/4" = 11 3/4", and 14 1/2" + 1 3/4" = 16 1/4".) You will need two pieces cut at each length you determine for your project. Miter both ends of each piece at 45°.

Test-fit the frame pieces around the backer board and adjust to fit. (See the drawing to the left where the backer board is shown with dashed lines.) Use glue to fasten corners of the frame. Clamp together until dry. Small brads can also be used to secure joints if desired.

Next, lay all the parts in their proper positions on the backer board. Remove one part at a time; apply glue to back side; and reposition onto backer board. (Do not glue the corner brackets in place until the frame has been attached to the backer board.) Before gluing the birds on, attach a length of cord or string to the heart, and wrap to form a knot-like area between the birds' beaks.

Attach backer board to frame. This can be installed permanently with glue and brads, or temporarily with clips or cleats.

Glue the corner brackets in place and attach a hanger to the back.

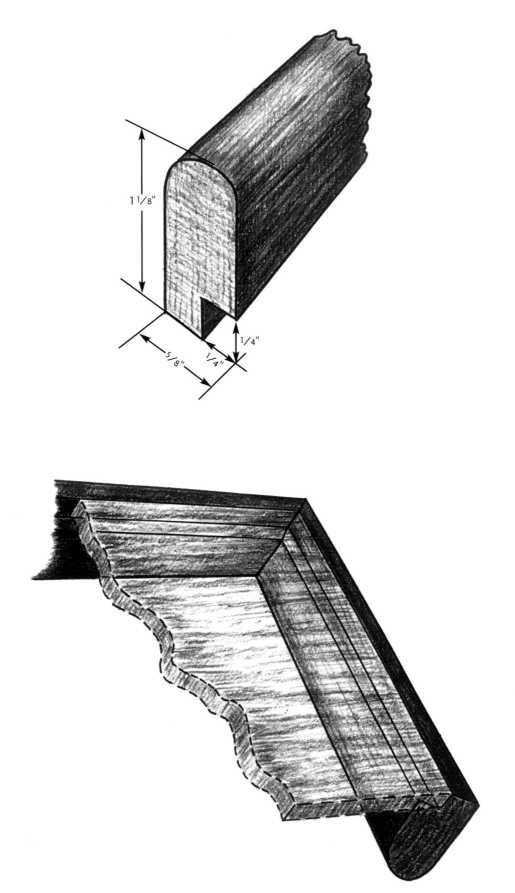

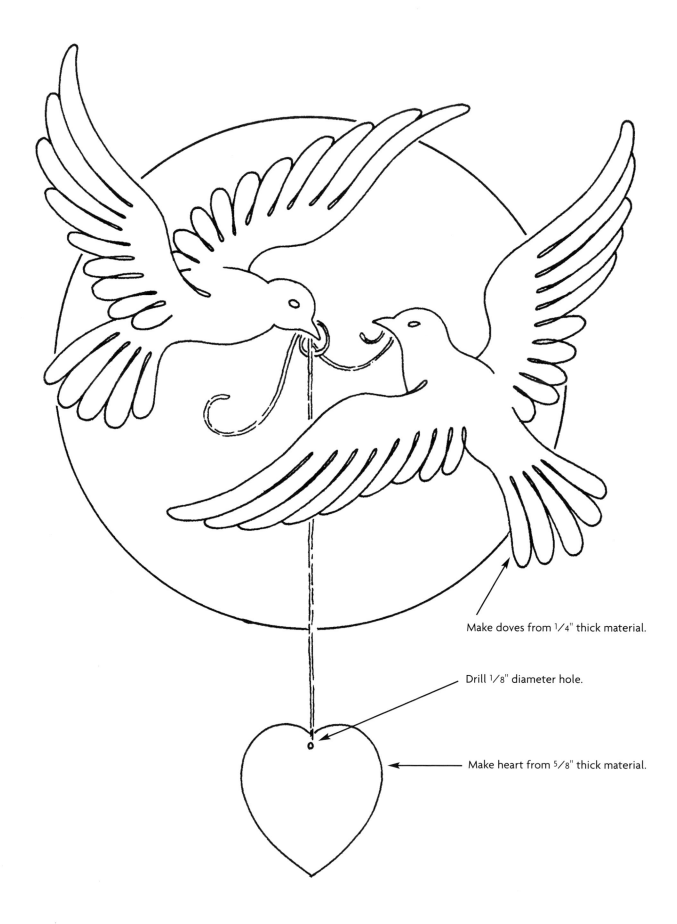

Make doves from 1/4" thick material.

Drill 1/8" diameter hole.

Make heart from 5/8" thick material.

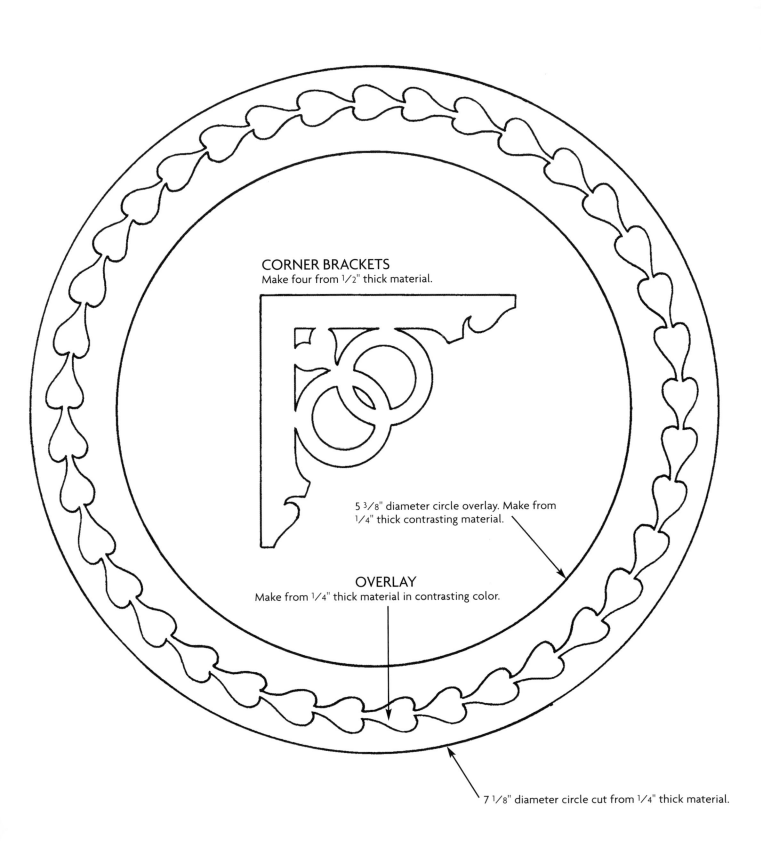

CORNER BRACKETS
Make four from 1/2" thick material.

5 3/8" diameter circle overlay. Make from 1/4" thick contrasting material.

OVERLAY
Make from 1/4" thick material in contrasting color.

7 1/8" diameter circle cut from 1/4" thick material.

Letters and Numbers

Make from 1/2" thick material.

"Painting" with Wood

Scroll saw segmentation portraiture is an exciting technique that involves a combination of fundamental scroll sawing and wood staining procedures. With it, any scroll saw artist capable of following a line can create realistic-looking, three-dimensional wooden portraits. The designs featured in this section are those of the artist Kerry Shirts, who has shown extensively in galleries in the western United States and whose work has sold internationally.

As with other scroll saw techniques, the sawing process involves temporarily bonding a photocopy of the pattern to the wood and sawing the individual pieces following the pattern lines. Next, the pieces are stained or colored according to the pattern, then reassembled and glued, being set at differing degrees of relief, to give the product texture and depth. As with an oil painting, a scroll-sawn wood portrait looks more realistic when viewed at a distance. Like brushwork on the canvas of a fine painting, details up close may not appear to make much sense; however, step back and the colors, tones, textures, and shadows merge into a wonderful, coherent image.

The majority of the patterns in this section will need to be enlarged with a photocopy machine. Where possible, enlargement recommendations given for the patterns are close to life-size, but you can make them any size desired. The projects range from elementary—involving just a few cut segments in simple shapes—to advanced projects with hundreds of pieces in highly detailed shapes. The procedures are essentially the same, the complex projects simply require more time. With the exception of the Fawn and the Leopard, very few inside cuts need to be made. Any size scroll saw capable of making consistently square, vertical cuts with commonly used blades is really the only tool necessary.

There are no hard and fast rules in the staining process. Patterns provide recommended staining instructions for coloring the individual pieces, but be aware that color intensity varies due to the absorbency levels of different woods. When finished, your project will not be an exact duplication of the photograph in the book. It will be your own creation, a one-of-a-kind piece of dramatic art that very likely neither you nor anyone else will be able to duplicate exactly again. Therein lies the enjoyment in making realistic scroll saw segmentation portraiture. What you are capable of producing with these basic techniques is virtually unlimited.

Applying the Pattern

Enlarge the pattern to the desired size, using a photocopy machine. Use scissors to remove the excess paper to within about 1/2" of the actual pattern (see photo). Make sure that the front surface of the wood is sanded and dust particles removed with a tack rag.

Apply a temporary bonding spray adhesive to the back of the pattern and hand-press the pattern onto the surface of the wood.

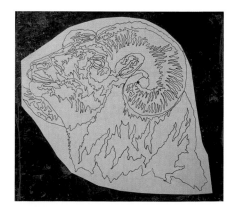

A photocopy of the pattern is trimmed with scissors and ready to apply to the wood.

Cutting the Wood

Preliminary practice cuts are recommended for beginners until lines can be followed consistently and confidence is gained. Patience and practice are the keys to developing sawing skills.

Beginners should also use the hold-down and guard. Making quick, sharp, "on the spot" turns to cut inside corners and acute angles requires practice and a fairly narrow blade.

For most projects, the pattern provides thin cutting lines to follow. Try to cut directly on the line. Cutting too far to one side of the line may spoil the integrity of the design. Avoid backing up and recutting a line if you happen to wander away from the line of cut. This only widens the saw kerf, which should be maintained as one continuous narrow width or the size of a single cut.

Some projects require making inside cuts. Simply drill a small hole through the work piece in an inconspicuous place. Thread the blade through the hole in the work piece, reattach it to the saw, and begin cutting.

Cut out the pattern segments, using the scroll saw (see photo). Use a medium (No. 5) or smaller (No. 2) blade as dictated by the amount of cutting detail and sharp radius turns required. Remember that all cuts must be perfectly vertical so the cut pieces can separate easily from the uncut segments.

Do not attempt to get extra use from a dull blade. Immediately change to a new blade at the first signs of charring in the cut. This will save you from immense frustration later. Dull blades tend to wander from the line of cut and make inclined cuts that are not vertical, resulting in beveled edges that interlock and refuse to separate.

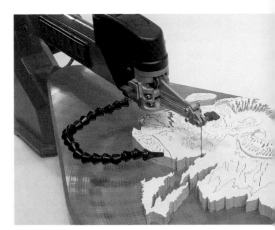

Typical portrait segments for the Big Horn Ram project are being cut. All pieces are sawn free, working from the outside inward. This and most other projects do not require making inside cuts.

Staining the Pieces

Staining is the second key element of the process. Staining can be as simple or as artistically complex and challenging as you wish to make it. Protective measures are recommended because staining can create quite a mess. Have wiping rags or paper toweling on hand to clean up spills and drips. Protect work areas with disposable papers, drop cloths, or plastic sheeting. Wear rubber gloves, if having stained hands is offensive, and wear a shop apron to protect clothing.

The staining process is not bound by rules. In fact, experimentation is strongly encouraged. There are, however, a few tips and suggestions that will be helpful. First, when cutting the individual segments free with the scroll saw, mark the back surface of each piece with an "X." This will keep the front surfaces properly oriented when staining and assembling the project.

Essentially, the object is to use just a few stains or coloring mediums creatively to achieve a wide range of color tones. These few might range from deep black to medium to a very light brown that still contrasts with the whiteness of the unfinished wood.

Just two stains, Golden Oak and Dark Walnut, are the primary colors used on every project. Disposable aluminum cake tins are great for dipping and slosh-staining with a foam brush.

Most of the recommended colors come from using just two basic stains: Golden Oak and Black or Dark Walnut stains (see photo). Other stain colors occasionally used for creating highlights and special effects are Red Mahogany and Salem Maple. For a jet-black look, apply a very heavy coat of Black Walnut stain and wait up to several days for it to dry, or simply use black liquid ink. The color intensity can be controlled somewhat by how the stain is applied and allowed to dry.

By mixing, layering, wiping, and smearing stains together, a near infinite variety and depth of color can be obtained.

Note: Generally, for these projects, unevenness in the application of stain is desirable. Very few things in nature are smooth and perfect; i.e., animal fur is not always groomed. Uneven effects look more like natural fur or feathers.

When the pattern key specifies, "Golden Oak mixed with Black Walnut," the two stains should be smeared together on the wood, not mixed together in a separate container. Mixing in a pan just creates another even shade. "Smear-mixing" can be done with a finger, the corner of a cloth rag, or with a cotton swab. Usually, it is best to smear Dark Walnut stain over the Golden Oak stain while it is still wet. Carefully study project photos; it can help determine which pieces have mixed colors and which do not.

Notice the color differences between two pieces of soft maple where one is stained Golden Oak and the other is left unstained.

Some lighter tones of Golden Oak stain on areas of certain pieces will also be noticeable. A soft, lightly colored effect is accomplished by wiping the surface immediately after the stain has been applied. This technique leaves just a little pigment on the wood—enough to contrast with the unstained pieces (see photo, right). With a little practice with a rag, it is possible to create a blend or faded effect on a highly visible segment. This technique has been effectively applied to the beak on the Vigilant Eagle Head on page 109.

Creating a Spotted Look

One method employed on the Fawn on page 108 and the Leopard on page 115 is to actually cut out the spots, or a series of connected spots, stain them separately, and reinsert them. This requires drilling a small blade-threading hole for every cutout. Spotted effects can also be created with contrasting drops or smudges of stain.

The spots on the Leopard are done by first applying a coat of Golden Oak stain; allowing it to partially dry (two to three hours); then, while it is still "tacky," using a small brush to daub on spots of the same Golden Oak stain.

Since oil and water do not mix, water is another method that can be used to create a spotting effect. Test this first on scrap. Apply the background stain as usual to the wood. While the stain is still wet, drip some water on it and "pat" it around with your finger so you do not have perfectly round drip spots. Once you have manipulated the water to spot or achieve the ruffled fur look you want, allow the piece to dry on a level surface.

Gluing the Assembly

The stained segments are assembled much like the pieces of a puzzle and then glued together. Some of these pieces are positioned higher and elevated above the surfaces of adjoining pieces to create a 3-D relief effect. See photos at right. The amount of relief can range from 1/16" to 3/16"—again there are no hard and fast rules.

The gluing is a very basic process. Simply lay a bead of carpenter's glue over the saw kerf on the back surface. See photo center right. Notice that we are not gluing for structural strength, but to maintain the relief level and to keep the pieces sticking to each other. The segments are not glued edge-to-edge as is done in conventional woodworking practices, common segmentation, or intarsia processes. The individual pieces are not glued to a backer either, although some could be. Later, entire portrait assemblies may or may not be glued to a backer, depending entirely on individual choice. Also, there are no shims glued under elevated segments, as is the practice in basic segmentation and intarsia work.

It may be best to glue separate sections of the portrait together before gluing others. Notice how all of the segments for the head of the Fawn were glued together as a single unit. The glue tends to run through wide saw kerf openings rather quickly, so turn the work front-side-up as soon as possible to prevent this from happening.

When viewing real life, the noses of animals and people are the closest to you. Therefore, gluing the nose segment farther out (higher in relief) than the eyes will make the project appear more realistic. Usually, but not always, darker stained pieces are shadows and they are glued farther back. White, unstained pieces represent highlights and these are usually (but not always) glued farther out, closer to the eye of the viewer. Side-by-side segments of the same stained color should alternate up and down slightly to cast small shadows to maintain relief and to give a textured look.

Here, two adjoining pieces are placed upside-down and positioned for gluing so the unstained piece will be about 1/16" to 1/8"

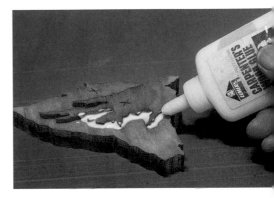

A bead fillet of glue being run along the saw cuts on the back surface. Notice the "X" marks that indicate the back surfaces.

Using Highlighting Techniques

In addition to "smear-mixing" and blending stains to create a realistic look on individual pieces, some additional highlighting can be added either before, during, or after gluing the assemblage of segments together. Just a little wipe of Salem Maple or Red Mahogany stain along one edge can have a dramatic effect (see photo, right). Also evident is the effective use of white paint to represent the glare glistening from a moist nose or to add realism to eyes. Very small dots can be applied with a toothpick or the pointed end of a small paintbrush handle.

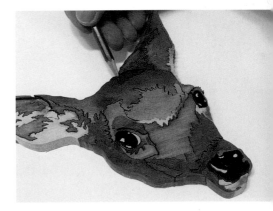

The piece between the ears has been smear-mixed with the addition of dark stain over the lighter. Notice the use of just a little Red Mahogany stain lightly wiped onto the unstained (white) segments in the ears, by the eyes, and just below the nose. Also note the use of white paint to make the eyes seem to glisten and the nose look moist.

Using Frames, Plaques, Backers & Display Props

There are numerous ways to display your completed "portrait." One is to frame it with a self-made or purchased molding (see photo at right). When framing, the portrait can be glued to a natural plywood backer that is unfinished, or whatever is desired. Usually, it is best to omit the placement of glass when framing.

Simple plaques with routed edges, such as the one developed for the Black Bear on page 111, are other alternatives. Notice the rustic log slab plaque for the mounting of the Vigilant Eagle (see photo at right).

Many of the projects are nicely displayed without any kind of visible plaque or backer. In such cases, it is best to cut a backer from a piece of 1/8" or 1/4" plywood slightly smaller (1/8" to 1/4") all around the profile outline of the portrait. Then glue the portrait to the backer, using construction-type gap-filling mastic or silicone adhesive. This adds to the structural integrity of the project without any visual distraction. The Big Horn Ram (below right and on page 113) is shown mounted to a simple painted plywood backer and a novel simulated stone plaque.

The Eagle Head (front view) is mounted on a rustic slab plaque.

The Fawn portrait is framed without glass.

Here, the Big Horn Ram is mounted on a simple, painted plywood plaque.

Making Simulated Stone Plaques

The simulated stone backer is a complementary way to mount wildlife portraits (see photo). A piece of 1/2" exterior plywood covered with 1/4" wire mesh provides the foundation for applying a home-use concrete patching mix. Cut the desired shape from the plywood and attach the wire mesh with a staple gun. Fold the edges over and attach to the back. Home-use concrete patching mix is available at local hardware stores and mixes with water. Wear rubber gloves and hand-smear the mixed patching compound onto the backer board.

While the mixture is still soft, stipple the surface with the bristle ends of a whisk broom to create a realistic-looking stone texture. When dry, attach the assembled wood portrait to the front surface with silicone, epoxy, or structural adhesive.

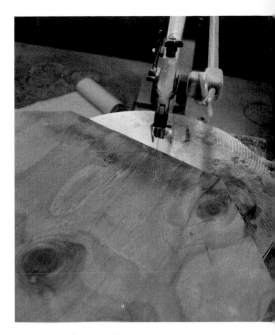

Cut a rough shape from inexpensive CD-grade plywood to make a simulated stone background plaque.

Attach 1/4" wire mesh to the plywood to serve as a reinforcement for the patching compound. Flatten the folded wire mesh to create natural-looking, irregular edges.

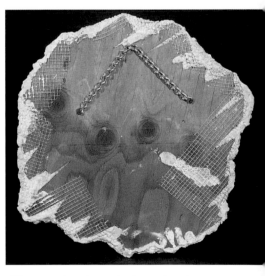

This rear view shows the heavy hanging chain and the edges of patching compound attached to the plywood with the "wrap" of wire mesh.

Beginner Projects
Sailboat

An easy piece to give you practice cutting. This project is 7" tall and has only 10 pieces.

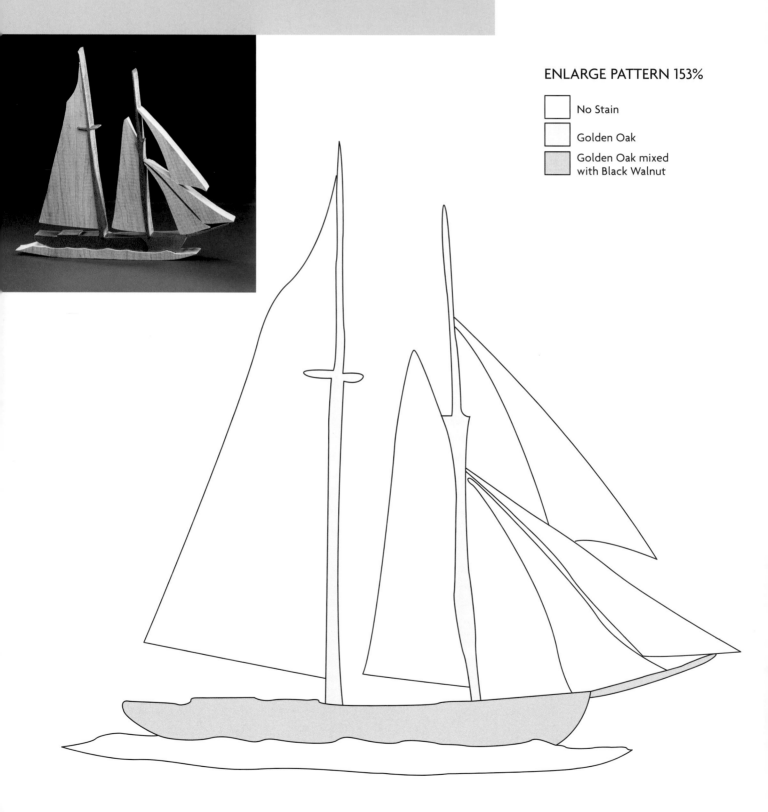

ENLARGE PATTERN 153%

☐ No Stain

☐ Golden Oak

▨ Golden Oak mixed with Black Walnut

Penguin

This has only 10 pieces and goes together quite quickly. The stomach does not need to be stained, which further simplifies this pattern. Maple wood makes a perfect contrast to the heavy dark walnut stain used for the back and the head. The pattern can be enlarged for a more life-sized creation.

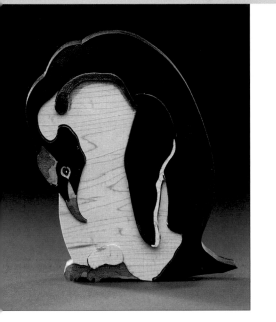

ENLARGE PATTERN 125%

☐ No Stain

☐ Golden Oak

▨ Black Walnut (heavy)

Paint white dot on eye. Refer to photograph for placement.

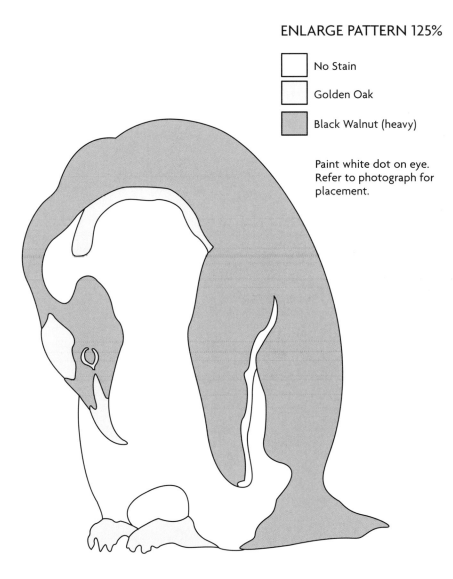

Songbird

This songbird, made up of 21 pieces, is quite a fun and simple pattern to cut out. If desired, you can make him larger or smaller. The enlargement recommended on the pattern is for a 10" model.

Begin by cutting the beak and then the eye and pupil. Continue to the neck and the crown of the head. The body is next and then the three sections of the wing. Move to the legs and the twig, and end by moving down from the top of the tail feathers.

ENLARGE PATTERN 117%

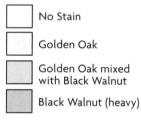

☐	No Stain
☐	Golden Oak
☐	Golden Oak mixed with Black Walnut
☐	Black Walnut (heavy)

Paint white dot on eye. Refer to photograph for placement.

Lighthouse Scene

People and animals are not the only things you can cut as portraits. This lighthouse is a delightful change of pace.

ENLARGE PATTERN 143%

No Stain

Golden Oak

Golden Oak mixed
with Black Walnut

Black Walnut (heavy)

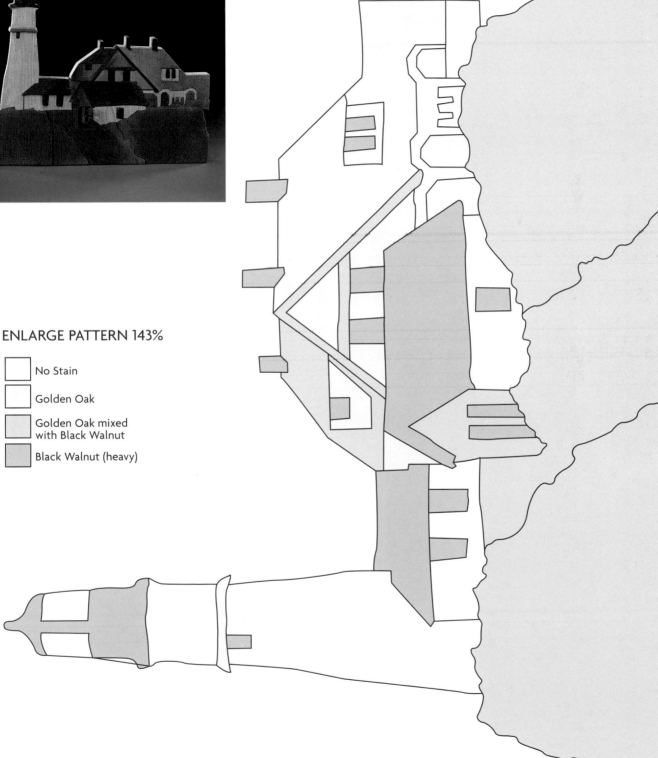

Kitty Cat

This simple kitty is approximately 8" square and is made up of 29 pieces.

ENLARGE PATTERN 167%

No Stain

Golden Oak

Golden Oak mixed with Black Walnut

Black Walnut (heavy)

Paint white dots on eyes. Refer to photograph for placement.

Puppy

A wonderful effect from only 24 pieces.

ENLARGE PATTERN 134%

- No Stain
- Golden Oak
- Black Walnut (wiped off)
- Golden Oak mixed with Black Walnut
- Black Walnut (heavy)

Paint white dots on eyes. Refer to photograph for placement.

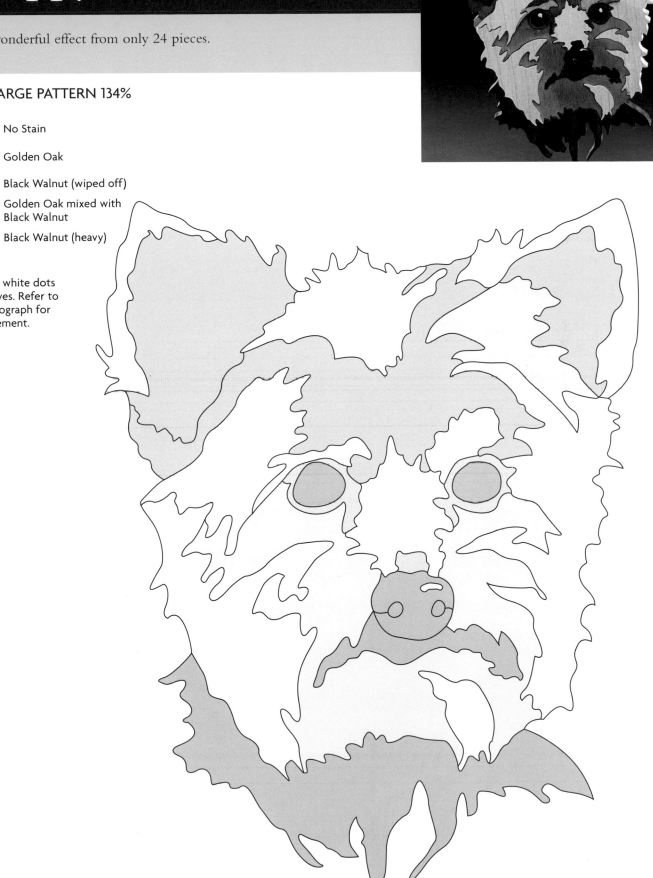

Fish

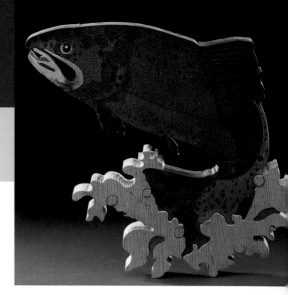

The leaping fish has lots of movement and drama for only 24 pieces.

ACTUAL SIZE PATTERN

No Stain

Golden Oak

Black Walnut (wiped off)

Golden Oak mixed with
Black Walnut

Paint white dot on eye.
Refer to photograph for
placement.

Howling Wolf

This project is approximately 10" tall and has only 24 pieces. It looks terrific on an oval backer after it's finished.

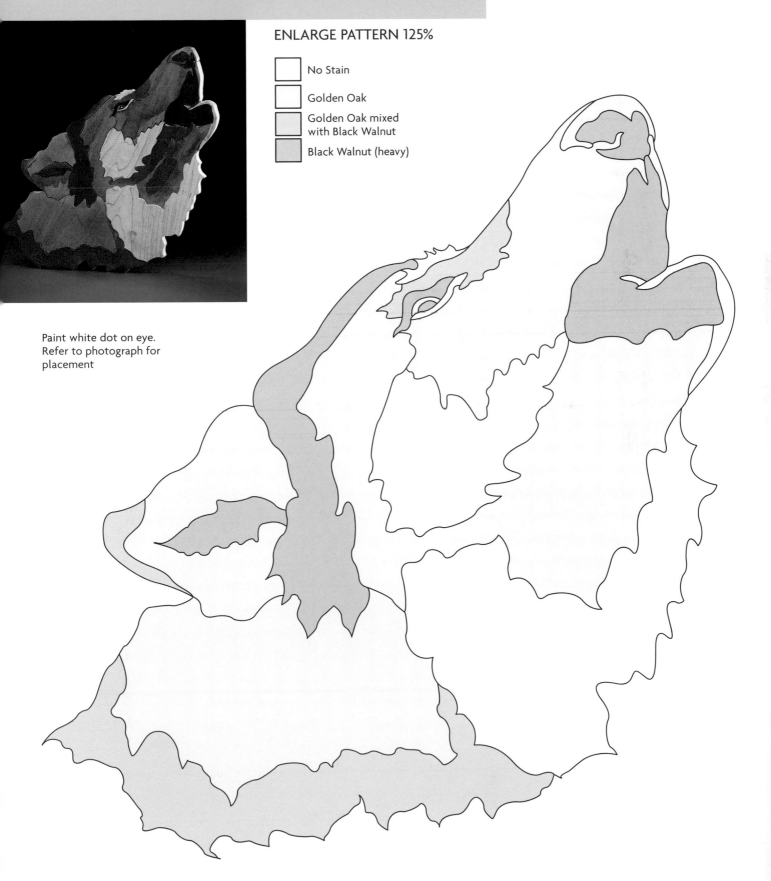

ENLARGE PATTERN 125%

No Stain

Golden Oak

Golden Oak mixed with Black Walnut

Black Walnut (heavy)

Paint white dot on eye. Refer to photograph for placement

Eagle Head Profile

A simple but realistic-looking eagle is approximately 6" square and is made up of just 16 pieces.

ENLARGE PATTERN 117%

- ☐ No Stain
- ☐ Golden Oak
- ☐ Golden Oak mixed with Black Walnut
- ☐ Black Walnut (heavy)

Paint white dot on eye. Refer to photograph for placement.

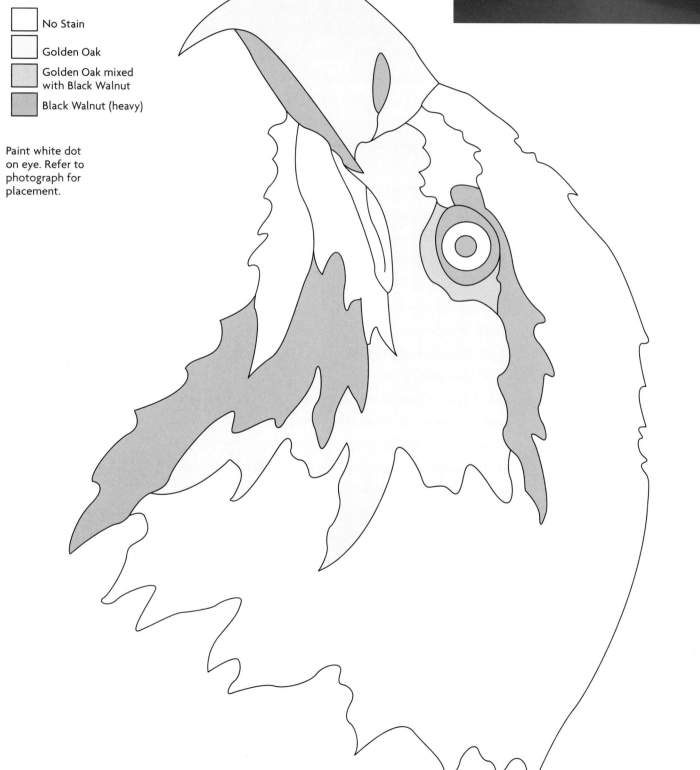

Zebra

One of the truly unique creatures on earth, this zebra can be cut larger if you prefer. He has 70 pieces but is really quite easy to cut, as he is mostly made up of stripes.

No Stain

Golden Oak

Golden Oak mixed with Black Walnut

Black Walnut (heavy)

ENLARGE PATTERN 117%

Paint white dot on eye. Refer to photograph for placement.

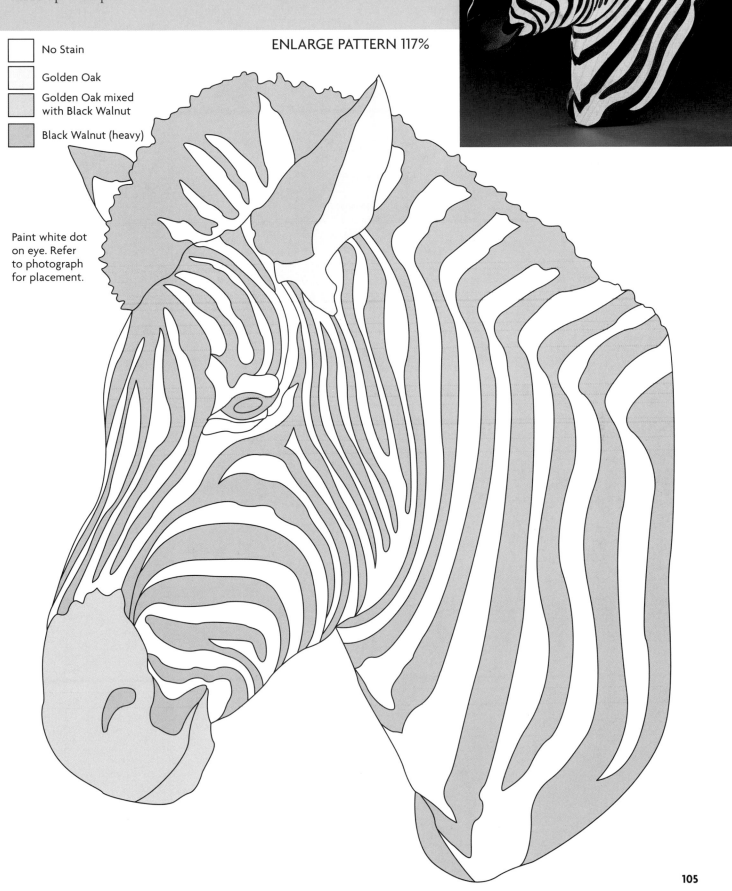

Chimp

An engaging chimpanzee is cut from an 8" square of wood and is made up of 31 pieces.

ENLARGE PATTERN 143%

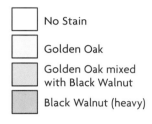

☐ No Stain

☐ Golden Oak

☐ Golden Oak mixed with Black Walnut

☐ Black Walnut (heavy)

Paint white dots on eyes. Refer to photograph for placement.

IntermediateProjects
Duck

Wood ducks have a lot of detail to show off. The actual size of this pattern is only 8" long, but you can cut him longer and larger.

ENLARGE PATTERN 117%

- [ ] No Stain
- [ ] Golden Oak
- [ ] Golden Oak mixed with Black Walnut
- [ ] Red Mahogany
- [ ] Black Walnut (heavy)

Paint white dot on eye. Refer to photograph for placement.

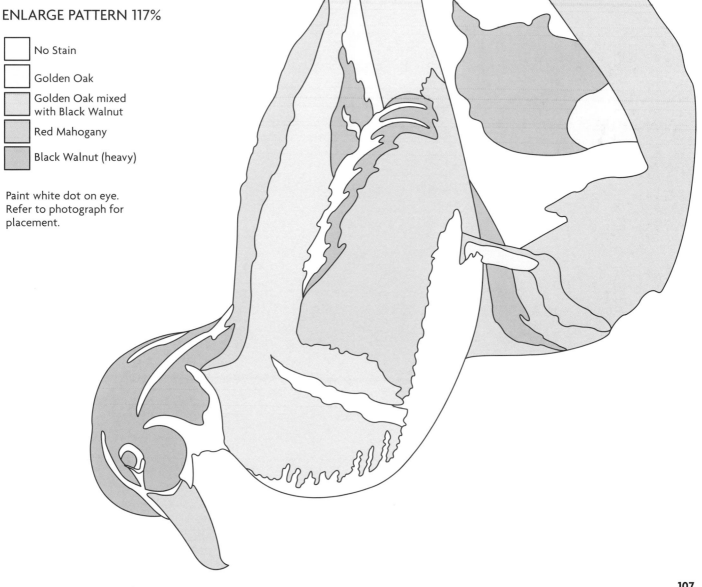

Fawn

For this piece you have to predrill blade entry holes before cutting the spots; otherwise, simple sawing is used throughout. The exciting thing is the opportunity to combine scrolling techniques to develop a piece of art. This framed project measures 17 1/2" by 16 1/4".

Paint white dots and curved lines on eyes and nose. Refer to photograph for placement.

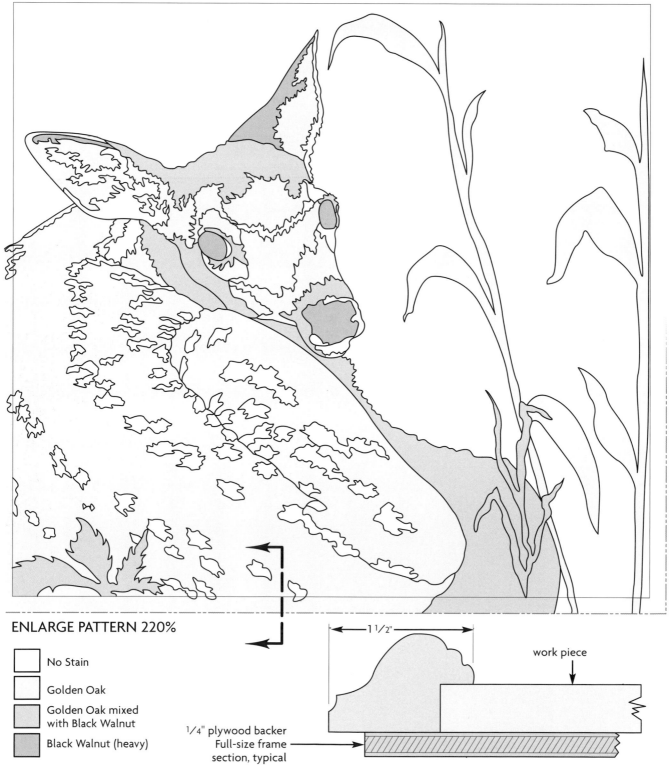

ENLARGE PATTERN 220%

- ☐ No Stain
- ☐ Golden Oak
- ☐ Golden Oak mixed with Black Walnut
- ☐ Black Walnut (heavy)

1 1/2"

work piece

1/4" plywood backer
Full-size frame
section, typical

Vigilant Eagle

ENLARGE PATTERN 143%

- ☐ No Stain
- ☐ Golden Oak
- ☐ Golden Oak mixed with Black Walnut
- ☐ Black Walnut (heavy)

Paint white dots on eyes. Refer to photograph for placement.

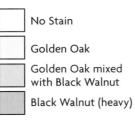

Staring Wolf

Paint white dots on eyes. Refer to photograph for placement.

ENLARGE PATTERN 111%

- No Stain
- Golden Oak
- Golden Oak mixed with Black Walnut
- Black Walnut (heavy)

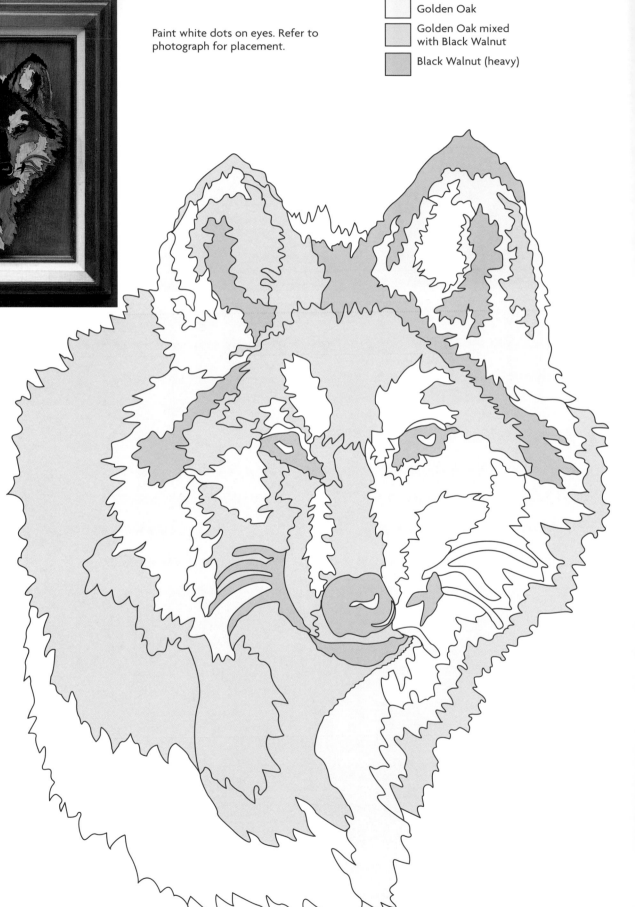

Black Bear

Oval plaque dimensions:
20¼" tall by 16½" wide.

Paint white dots on eyes.
Refer to photograph for
placement.

ENLARGE PATTERN 143%

☐ No Stain

☐ Golden Oak

☐ Golden Oak mixed
with Black Walnut

☐ Black Walnut (heavy)

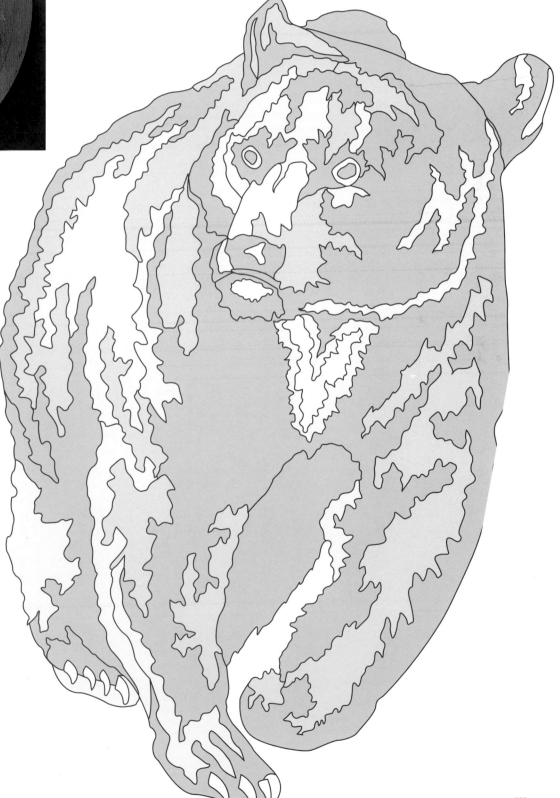

Lion Head

Excellent detail can result from using a No. 2 scroll saw blade and being very patient. It is best to go about half speed with this blade, causing less breakage. Glue the lion's lower body back farthest, with his mane flaring out. The white chin is closest to you, so it is glued the farthest out.

ENLARGE PATTERN 167%

- No Stain
- Golden Oak
- Black Walnut (wiped off)
- Golden Oak mixed with Black Walnut
- Black Walnut (heavy)

Paint white dots on eyes. Refer to photograph for placement.

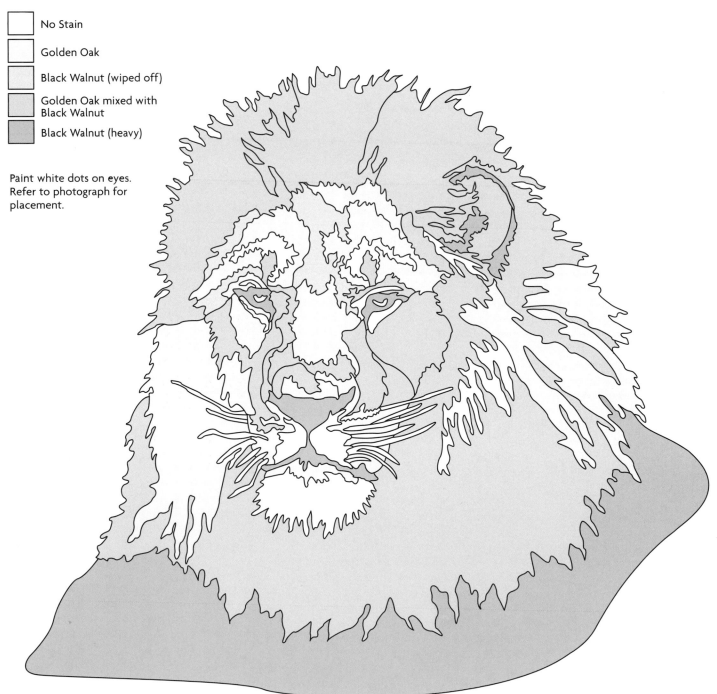

Expert Projects
Big Horn Ram

This Big Horn Ram is approximately 10" square and mounted on a simulated stone plaque. The curly maple used actually adds to its dimensionality.

ENLARGE PATTERN 167%

☐ No Stain

☐ Golden Oak

▨ Golden Oak mixed with Black Walnut

▨ Black Walnut (heavy)

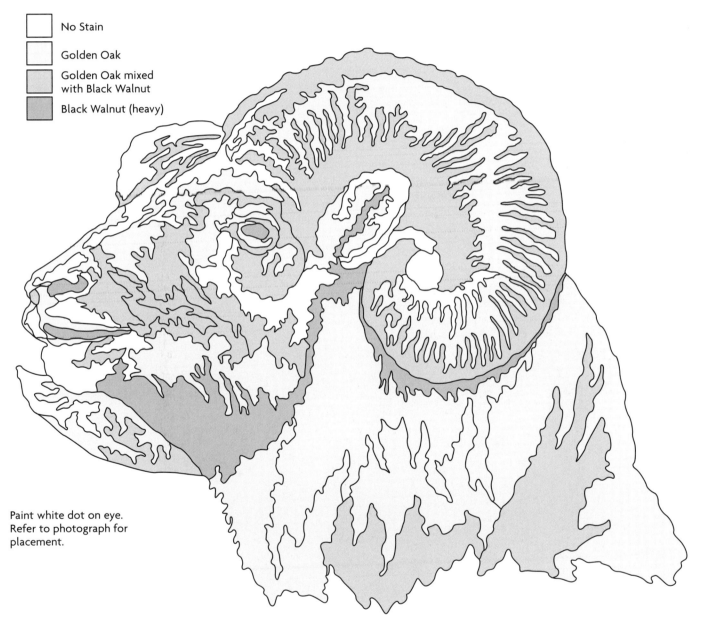

Paint white dot on eye. Refer to photograph for placement.

PLAQUE PATTERN
ENLARGE 286%

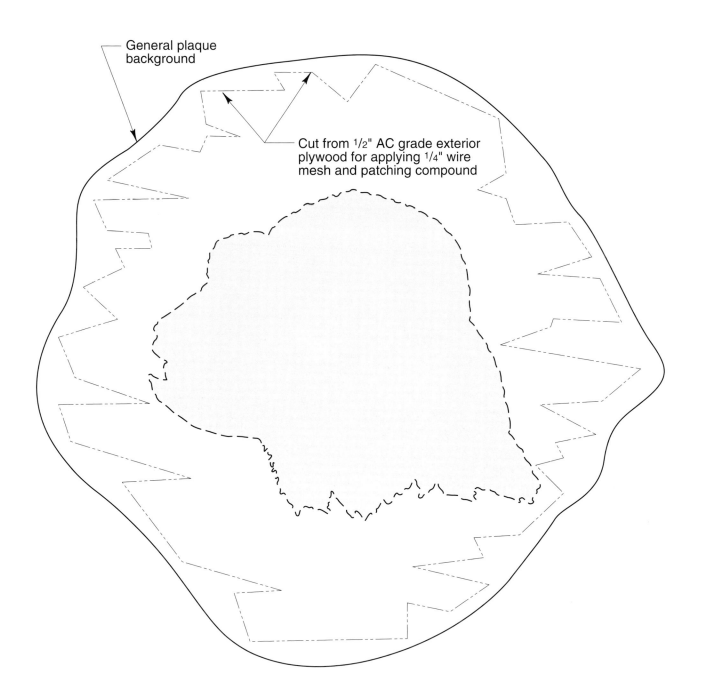

General plaque
background

Cut from ¹/₂" AC grade exterior
plywood for applying ¹/₄" wire
mesh and patching compound

Leopard

ENLARGE PATTERN 285%

- ☐ No Stain
- ☐ Golden Oak
- ☐ Black Walnut(wiped off)
- ☐ Golden Oak mixed with Black Walnut
- ☐ Black Walnut (heavy)

Paint white dots on eyes. Refer to photograph for placement.

This portrait technique makes the eyes look like glass. Cut this cat quite large so that details can be cut into his eyes (see close-up photo). His finished size is 16" by 22". The eyes require a $3/64$" blade entry hole and all fine details are cut with a No. 2 blade. The white part of the eye is intricate. Cut it on a rather slow speed so that it can be cut in one piece.

You don't have to cut each and every spot to have them appear dramatic. Combined spots can still look like individual spots.

Predrill a blade hole for each separate spot on the left side of the face. After you stain them heavily with dark walnut, the drill holes will not show. Stain the pieces as you cut them, so that the stain can dry as you continue cutting. Keep them all together in a group so that

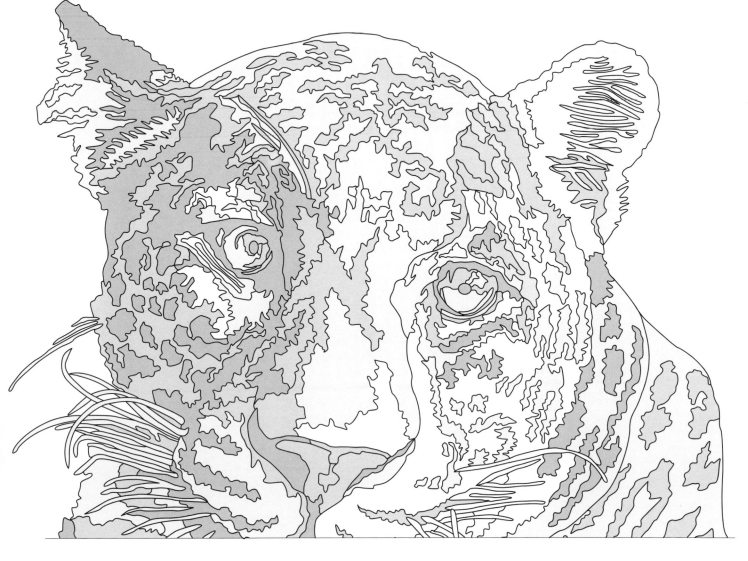

you don't mix up spots from other areas of his body. This will make assembly infinitely easier. Also predrill the spots in his forehead and eyebrows.

For the chin, cut out the spots first, stain them according to the pattern, and then cut the whiskers and the rest of the chin. Leave the whiskers unstained or brush them with golden oak stain and then wipe them off to keep them a lighter color.

The body is cut and stained a very dark golden oak. Give it three applications to deepen the golden color of his coat. The spots are stained golden oak with a mix of black walnut.

After the piece is assembled and glued, drop golden oak stain on the already stained body. This stain on stain looks like additional spots on the golden coat, and adds even more dimension.

Scrolling and Sculpting

Introduction to Scrolling and Sculpting

This section covers a craft, called "segmentation" by its inventor, that can be learned in a reasonably short time by anyone with a knowledge of basic scroll saw skills. The fine-line cutting capability of the scroll saw is used in combination with some elementary wood-shaping techniques to make pieces that appear to be artfully carved. These sculptural-looking works appear to require much more advanced and masterful skills than they actually do.

The essential techniques of scroll saw segmentation were introduced more than 12 years ago by Patrick Spielman, award-winning author of more than 60 woodworking books, editor of the bimonthly magazine, *Home Workshop News*, and co-owner with his wife of the gift galleries, Spielman's Wood Works and Spielman's Kid Works.

Segmentation versus Intarsia

Segmentation is sometimes referred to as "painted intarsia." Intarsia is also called "3-D marquetry," or "3-D inlay." The techniques involved are very similar. Both segmentation and intarsia impart a visual effect of low-relief carving, and both can be carried to various levels of sophistication (or difficulty) to create beautiful flat-backed sculptures. Cutting a design into segments, contouring each segment with hand or power tools, applying finish, then reassembling and gluing the segments together again results in a piece that emulates fine carving, but the work is much easier to accomplish.

The main difference between segmentation and intarsia is that segmentation projects, as a rule, use a single piece of inexpensive material from which all segments of the design are cut and shaped. A pigmented stain, paint, or natural finish is then applied to the segments before reassembly. There are many finishing and painting options available for segmentation projects.

For intarsia, on the other hand, each segment is cut individually from wood chosen specifically for its natural color and grain, with clear finishes applied to show off these wood characteristics as part of the design. Intarsia is more labor-intensive and somewhat more difficult to accomplish. As the parts are not all cut from a single piece of wood, every segment must be carefully shaped to fit precisely against the one it will adjoin. In addition, many species of wood may be required to supply the colors and textures to fulfill the design. You will be selecting stock from many pieces of wood in different natural colors, therefore using more expensive material. For example, walnut and maple provide dark brown and white that may be combined with various pink shades of Western cedar to create a colorful palette (see photo at right).

Shaping and Smoothing the Segments

In segmentation work, after preparation of the wood and cutting out the pattern (reviewed in Basics on pages 7 and 8), there are various fundamental shaping requirements for the individual segments. Most projects involve chamfered or rounded-over edges.

Some projects, however, will look more interesting if formed to tapered, concave, or convex surfaces before working the edges. Most wood-workers probably already have their own favorite devices or tools they like to use to shape wood. Choose one or a combination of the following techniques.

Segmentation projects are shown with an all-natural finish (left) and some segments stained (right).

Here, segmentation finishing incorporates a variety of options: natural, stained, and colored with acrylic paints. See pages 151-152 for Rooster Plaques patterns.

As shown in the designs and work of noted intarsia artist Lucille Crabtree, selecting varieties of different wood species provides an all-natural wood palette.

Finger-gauge a line to guide the round-over of an edge.

Where different levels or thicknesses exist, shape the lower segments first. Draw guide lines on adjoining segments to facilitate contouring so they appear to flow together as if carved from one piece.

Shaping with Hand Tools

Use sandpaper wrapped around a thin wooden tongue depressor, a dowel, or a pencil for minimal edge shaping and most smoothing jobs.

Use files, rasps, carving knives, and chisels to round-over cut edges or for giving other shapes to cut segments.

Sandpaper wrapped around a tongue depressor makes an effective file for rounding over edges of concave curves and in tight areas.

Sandpaper around a dowel or any round object, such as a pencil, is useful for rounding over edges of concave curves.

Rubbing an edge of a segment against a 60- or 80-grit abrasive held over a padded corner of the workbench will round-over and smooth small segments nicely.

A rasp, a file, or a knife may be used to carve in detail, such as the mouth for the Striped Fish (see project on page 134).

Use a knife to shape MDF (medium density fiberboard) to a sharply rounded inside corner for the Unicorn's eye (see project on page 166).

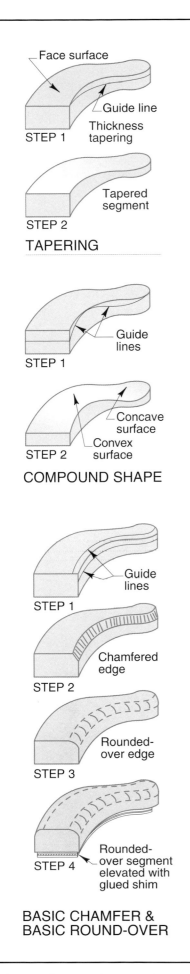

Face surface
Guide line
Thickness tapering
STEP 1

Tapered segment
STEP 2

TAPERING

Guide lines
STEP 1

Concave surface
Convex surface
STEP 2

COMPOUND SHAPE

Guide lines
STEP 1

Chamfered edge
STEP 2

Rounded-over edge
STEP 3

Rounded-over segment elevated with glued shim
STEP 4

BASIC CHAMFER & BASIC ROUND-OVER

These are the essential steps to shaping the edges of segments.

Shaping with Rotary Tools

Use high-speed rotary tools to tackle a variety of shaping and surface detailing jobs. Various accessories in different profiles and sizes are available for abrasive cutting and grinding of wood.

Use innovative methods to safely hold very small segments for edge or surface shaping with hand and/or power tools. Use pliers or temporarily adhere the segment to a holding stick (dowel) with hot glue or double-sided tape. Obviously, you cannot safely hold small segments with your fingers.

Hold a small thin segment with side-cutting pliers while rounding the edges by hand with an abrasive.

Round-over an edge with a small, coarse-grit sanding drum.

Carve a surface depression with a structured carbide burr.

An inexpensive hand drill stand makes a good shaping and smoothing center for using drum sanding accessories if a drill press is not available.

Needle-nose pliers grip a small segment while it is shaped on a supporting block with a rotary tool.

Temporarily bond the segment to a holding stick with double-sided tape or hot glue as the segment is worked against a drill press drum sander.

Shaping with Small Routers

Use a small trim router to round over segmented edges quickly and uniformly.

Use bits from a 1/8" to a 3/8" radius.

Use the pattern on the opposite page for making your own zero-clearance router base.

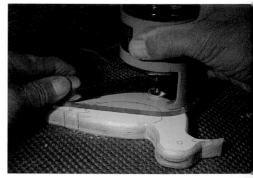

Round over on a non-slip router pad. Here, all the outside edges of this profile are rounded over before the smaller integral segments are cut free into smaller, separate, segments. Then the smaller segments are rounded over by hand.

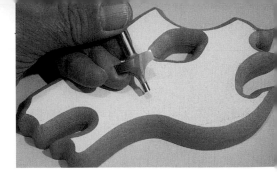

This carbide-tipped router bit has a small brass pilot that is only 5/32" in diameter, perfect for getting into tight corners. It cuts the MDF (medium density fiberboard) Unicorn head (page 166) without dulling.

Look closely at the shop-made plastic router base. Note that the hole for the bit has almost zero-clearance around it, which is essential to support the router when rounding over small segments.

Right: This full-size pattern is typical for a trim router base.

Round over a medium- to small-sized segment with a small trim router. Note the special shop-made, clear plastic base. Pressure is maintained downward during the cut, forcing the work piece tightly against the non-slip router pad. Perform this operation with caution. Wear suitable eye and hearing protection.

Right: A small Dremel rotary tool also equipped with a near zero-clearance plastic base for use with a small round over bit.

Applying Texture to Segments

Use a wood-burning tool for texturing and quickly producing v-cut lines into surfaces to simulate detail, such as hair. Produce other textured surfaces that might be more difficult to create with files or carving knives.

Left: A wood-burning tool is ideal for adding definition lines to accent various surfaces of individual segments.

Reducing Segment Thickness

Sometimes it is recommended that certain segments be reduced in thickness. This task can be done in various ways, but sawing and abrasive cutting are the two easiest options.

Use the flat surfaces of belt sanders or disk sanders with coarse abrasives, 36 to 50 or 60 grit, for quick flat, parallel, or tapered-thickness stock removal. Reduce thickness by removing material from the face, or front surface, of the segment. Removing stock from the surface that will be glued to the backer is not a good practice. If you should inadvertently remove material unevenly, or taper the surface, the edges will not fit as tightly as they should to the adjoining segments. Where thickness reduction is required, it will be indicated on the project pattern with a minus (-) sign.

Small segments can be cut to a desired thickness with the scroll saw.

A disk sander accessory made from plywood for the lathe will do many of the same jobs as belt sanding machines.

To taper two sides of a segment, use a 6" vertical belt sanding machine.

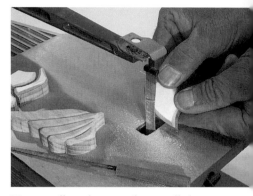

Use a scroll sander to produce small chamfered edges on ash segments.

Shimming Segments

Glue a shim to the back side of certain inside segments to slightly raise the segments. This technique adds to the relief. A segment representing a nose, for example, can make a face appear more realistic if raised just 1/8" above the surrounding segments. Where a shim is required, it will be indicated on the project pattern with a plus (+) sign.

Smoothing with Scroll Sanders

Use scroll sanders, available in several grit sizes, with the scroll saw to smooth segments that have already been shaped. Scroll sanders also work well to soften sharp edges or where little wood removal is required. Emery boards (fingernail files) are also useful in the shop. Use them to make your

Make your own scroll sanders from emery boards (fingernail files). If necessary, cut them to length and use super glue or epoxy to adhere them onto used or dull scroll saw blades.

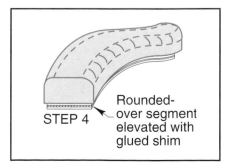

STEP 4

Rounded-over segment elevated with glued shim

Smoothing with Pneumatic and Soft Drum Sanders

Use pneumatic and soft drum sanders for shaping segmentation and intarsia projects. The pneumatic drums have the advantage of being inflated to the desired pressure to match the work piece being sanded. The pneumatic type, available from Woodcraft, measures 3" in diameter x 8" in length and can be mounted in a lathe or in a drill press. The less expensive "Flex Drum" sander, manufactured by Seyco Sales Co., attaches to a 1725 rpm motor shaft or to a drill press. The foam-supported abrasive of the flex drum sander is not adjustable as far as hardness is concerned, but it is designed with a medium pliability intended specifically for intarsia work.

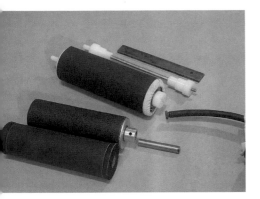

A pneumatic (air filled) drum sander rotates between the centers of a lathe or can be driven vertically in a drill press (top). An ordinary bicycle tire pump provides the air. A less expensive foam-cushioned sander is designed specifically for contour sanding of segmented and intarsia pieces (bottom).

Smoothing with Orbital Sanders and Flutter Wheels

Smooth the segments, using a powered device, such as a small orbital hand-held sander. Use flutter abrasive wheels of 150 or 180 grit for smoothing all kinds of contour surfaces. These drill accessories allow sanding of small segments without injury to your fingers should you get them too close.

The foam-cushioned sander is designed to mount onto a 1/2" or 5/8" motor shaft. It can also be installed in the drill press.

Small hand-held electric sanders work well for sanding flat and convex surfaces.

Flutter wheels of 150 and 180 grit will smooth most any surface contour.

Color & Finish the Segments

Use oil stains, natural finishes, opaque colored paints, or transparent colored dyes and colored stains. To assure a good glue bond, do not finish concealed gluing areas along the edges or the backs of segments.

Note: Always test whatever finish you choose for a project on scrap material first, to assure that it will deliver the look that you want before applying it to your project.

Use water-based acrylic paint to color the individual shaped segments. Note that all of the non-visible gluing surfaces at the edges are left unpainted to insure a good glue bond.

Transparent colors are very effective and yield interesting results as they do not conceal the wood's figure, or grain. When using water-based dyes, first sponge-dampen the surfaces. Allow to dry. Sand the surfaces with the grain to remove the raised grain. Then moisten the wood and wipe out with the grain again just before the dye is applied. Create lighter shades by diluting the dye pigment with water. Watered-down acrylic paints also can be used to suggest color, yet still allow the wood grain to show through.

An oil-based, colored stain product is available that is much easier to apply than water-based dyes. It is a tung oil finish with pigments that imitate a dye. To use this product, simply wipe it on the dry, sanded wood with paper towels.

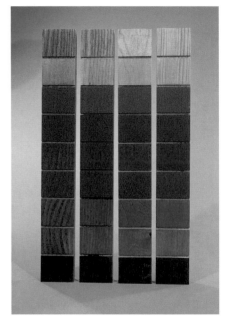

Concentrated water-based dyes are commonly used to color wood.

Colored stains are easy-to-use (but more expensive) products that are applied to dry, raw wood with paper towels.

Natural, light-colored woods take water-based wood dye colors best. Woods, left to right: oak, ash, birch, and pine.

Assemble the Segments

Place a pattern photocopy on a clean, flat surface. Cover it with waxed paper or freezer paper that is fairly transparent. You can also use plastic wrap. Glue the segments together at the edges, using the adhesive of your choice. Yellow carpenter's glue and instant/super glues are recommended because they set fairly quickly.

Make a Backer

Reassemble the segments and glue them together at the edges to make the whole again.

Carefully lay the assembled segments on a piece of 1/8" to 1/4" plywood and trace the outline shape of the project. Cut a backer piece from the plywood. Glue the backer to the assembled segments. Attach a sawtooth picture hanger to projects that are to be hung on the wall.

For one-sided, wall-hanging projects, trace around the assembly onto a 1/8" or 1/4" plywood backer.

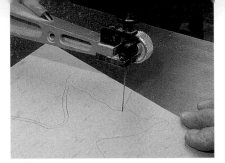

With the saw table tilted 15° to 20°, cut 1/8" inside the layout line to make the backer.

Use spring clamps or weights to hold the backer to the pre-glued segments. Notice the tenon, shown at the pencil point, which will fit into a base, making this particular project free-standing.

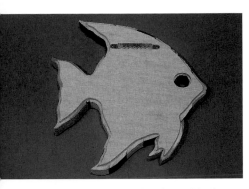

This rear view shows the plywood backer and a sawtooth picture hanger, which is typical of all wall-hanging segmentation pieces.

Shown are two methods of perfecting the roped edge, using two types of rope: sisal-hemp rope on the left with a retwisting technique appears seamless. The nylon rope on the right has a simple glued butt joint that is barely visible. The pencils point to rope ends.

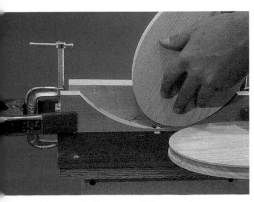

Rout a shallow round-bottomed groove around the edge of the plaque to "seat" the rope, using a router table.

Rope-edged Plaques

The rope-edging technique can be used to embellish nautical plaques, western plaques and various signs. If the rope ends are crudely butted, rope-edged plaques can look shoddy. Here are two different techniques for perfecting rope edging on plaques, using two kinds of rope. One method magically conceals the rope ends, making the rope look seamless. This technique is more involved than the other, but it is certainly worth the extra effort.

Ropes

Most hardware stores sell three types of rope: 1) sisal hemp rope; 2) white nylon rope; and 3) yellow polypropylene rope. Ropes are also either twisted or braided. Avoid polypropylene and braided ropes. Select a rope size (diameter) that complements the thickness of the wooden plaque. For example, use 5/8" rope with 3/4" plaques. If mounted flush to the front surface of the plaque, 3/4" or 1/2" rope also will work.

Preparing the Plaques

1. Cut boards to round or oval shapes. Round the corners on square, triangular, or other geometric shapes so the rope does not have to make a sharp bend.

2. Using a 5/8" diameter round-nose bit and a router table, rout a 1/8" deep groove into the edge of the plaque to cradle the rope. See the detail of the rope-edged section on the Mermaid pattern on page 139. This groove will accommodate 1/2" to 3/4" diameter rope.

3. Clamp a concave-edged board to the fence to support the work piece over the bit, assuring a uniform depth of cut.

4. Slightly offset the groove toward the front of the plaque. Rout with the front surface facing away from the fence and keep the stock moving into the bit.

5. Clamp a piece of thin plywood to a table that has a zero-clearance hole surrounding the bit. This will help when routing edge grooves on rounded corners and connecting straight edges of square and rectangular plaques.

As an alternative, shallow v-grooves can be fabricated around plaque edges by gluing two pieces of wood, back to back, that have previously bevel-cut edges. Upon completion of the process, an inverted v-edge will have been formed all around.

Chamfering & Finishing

1. Chamfer the edge on the back of the plaque next to the groove when pre-made loops of rope will be stretch-fit into the grooves. See the detail of the rope-edged section on the Mermaid pattern on page 139. Plaques roped with butted ends do not require chamfering.

2. Completely finish plaques before applying the rope edging. Leave surfaces of the groove unfinished where you may want to glue the rope into the groove.

The secret to eliminating fraying and un-raveling is to plasticize the rope with an instant glue before cutting it. Notice how the nylon strands lose their shape compared to those of the sisal rope when untwisted.

Preparing the Rope

For convenience sake, the two different techniques for mounting rope to plaque edges have been named as "glue-butting" and "re-twisting." Each technique requires different preparation. Both nylon and sisal ropes can be used for the glue-butting technique, but only sisal rope works well for the re-twisting process. A thin-consistency instant glue is necessary for the glue-butting method and helpful for the re-twisting technique.

Cut the rope on the scroll saw. A thin board taped to the table supports the rope over the table opening around the blade.

Glue-butting

Just as the name implies, the rope is glued end-to-end with instant glue. This method leaves a visible glue line, but is the quickest and easiest technique for both sisal and nylon ropes. The key is to keep the ends from fraying.

1. Using a clear, low-viscosity, instant adhesive, saturate the cutting areas. See photo, top right.

Note: The adhesive sets in a few seconds, allowing the rope to be cut on the scroll saw without fraying. Using the adhesive to plasticize the rope allows you to work it almost like wood or plastic.

Mark the rope where ends butt.

2. Square one end of the rope. Measure, mark, cut, square to length, and assemble. See photos, center right.

3. Apply a gap-filling instant glue or epoxy into the plaque groove. Place one end of the rope into the glue-filled groove. Tightly pull the other end to it, matching the twists of the rope, and glue the joint. Note: A gap-filling instant glue is ideal for this job because it sets quick. It is best to locate the butt joint at the bottom of the plaque where light shadows will help to hide the joint.

This piece of nylon rope has sharp, clean, and square cuts, making it ready for gluing end to end.

The rope now has a glued-butt joint. Use a craft knife to cut away any glue "squeeze out" and to shape the joint.

Shown here is a completed butt joint on sisal rope.

A length that is three times the circumference is required.

Re-twisting

This technique requires three times the amount of rope to edge one plaque, but it creates a wonderful-looking edge that appears to be seamless. Although this method is not difficult, it is recommended to make some practice loops first.

Use sisal rope and select one with strands that hold their shape well when separated. Nylon strands become very limp and flimsy when separated, making a neat re-twisting job impossible.

1. Measure the length of rope required to encircle your plaque. Mark clearly around all three strands of the rope at this point.

2. Cut the rope to three times this measured length.

Note: It helps to give the rope a light dose of thin instant glue at the cut ends so the strand ends still separate from each other but do not fray or unravel.

3. Now untwist the rope into three individual strands.

4. Starting at the previously marked one-third point of the total length, re-twist one strand to form a two-strand loop. It is helpful to place a drop of glue at this point, under the starting end.

5. Tightly and uniformly pull the two strands in the loop together as you continue to re-twist the strands, forming a two-strand loop.

6. Continue retwisting around the loop until you have created a three-strand loop of rope

7. Prepare the plaque with a shallow groove. Be certain to chamfer the back edge to facilitate stretching the rope onto the edge of the plaque.

8. Stretch the loop onto the plaque. If the loop is too large you can undo it and start again. If the loop is too small you can reduce the size of the plaque until it fits.

Retwist one strand to make what appears to be an endless loop of three-strand rope.

The completed loop of twisted rope has only the ends of one of the three new strands butting together, which can be concealed against the wood in the groove.

Using two screwdrivers for leverage, force a rope loop onto a plaque with the plaque face down.

Nautical Themes

Shore Bird

SUPPLIES

3/8" Baltic birch plywood: 3" x 7"

5/8" pine: 2¼" x 2¼"

3/16" doweling: 5 ½" long

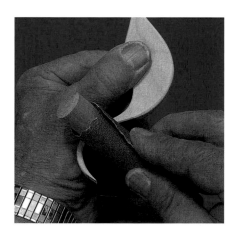

INSTRUCTIONS

1. Apply one Shore Bird pattern from page 129 to Baltic birch plywood.

1. Cut out the outside profile of the bird.

2. Drill a 3/16" hole ½" deep in the bottom segment of the bird for the dowel.

3. Cut out the segments; cut out the base from pine. Drill the eye hole and a hole through the center of the base (see photo, top right).

4. Slightly chamfer the edges along the glue line between the two segments (see photo, bottom right).

5. Color, finish and assemble the segments. Apply wood glue to both ends of the dowel. Insert the dowel into the base and bottom segment.

Above: The Shore Bird is shown with the segments and parts cut out.

Left: Use 80-grit abrasive over a dowel to chamfer the edges along the glue joint.

FULL-SIZE PATTERN

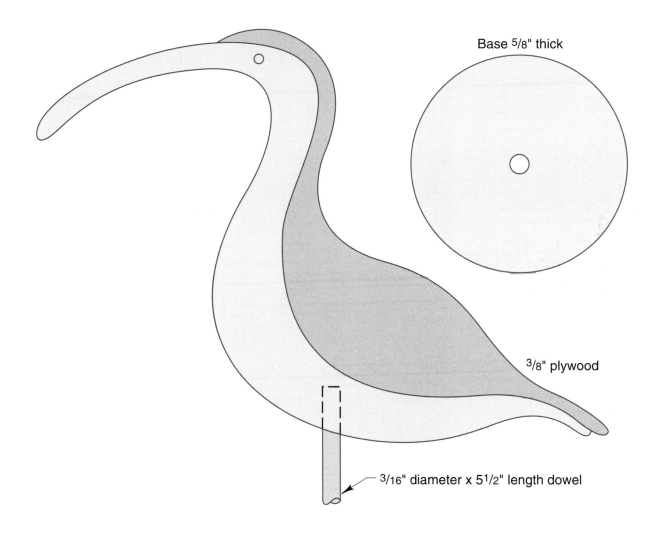

Base 5/8" thick

3/8" plywood

3/16" diameter x 5 1/2" length dowel

Sea Gull

SUPPLIES

3/4" clear pine: 4" x 7 1/4"

3/4" pine: 2" x 3"

INSTRUCTIONS

1. Apply one Sea Gull pattern from page 131 to clear pine.

2. Cut out the outside profile of the bird.

3. Make two cuts along the bill, partway in from the outside, but do not cut the bill free—leave about 1/8" of the line uncut (see photo, below right).

4. Round-over the entire outside profile (including the bill) on the front and the back to a 3/16" radius.

5. Drill a 1/4" hole about 1/2" deep in the bottom of the bird for the dowel (see photos, opposite page).

6. Cut out the segments, including the remainder of the bill. Cut the base from the 5/8" pine. Drill the eye hole and a hole through the center of the base.

7. Color, finish, and assemble the segments. Apply wood glue to both ends of the dowel. Insert the dowel into the base and the bottom of the bird.

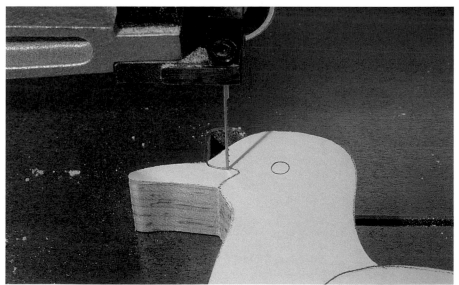

Right: Do not cut the bill free until after rounding over the entire outside profile. Here, one cut is made partway inward from the outside edge before rounding over.

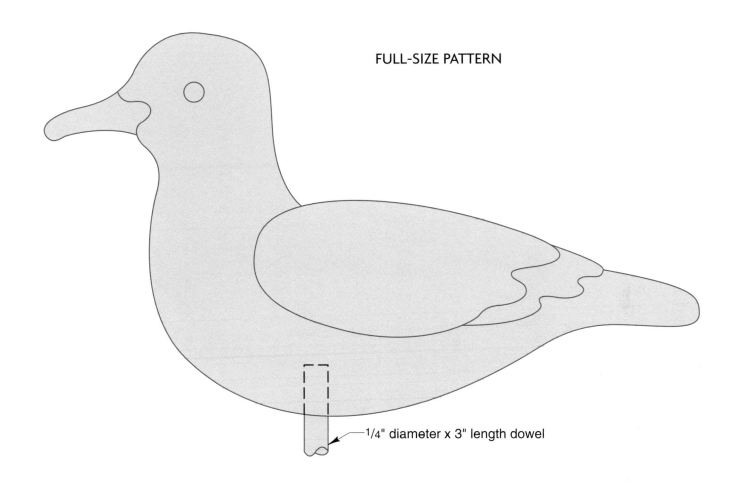

FULL-SIZE PATTERN

¹/4" diameter x 3" length dowel

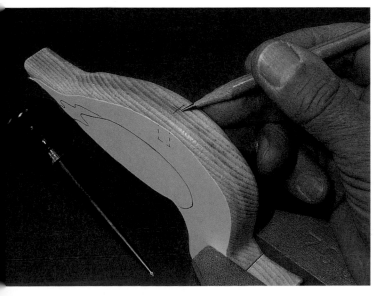

Here, all the outside edges have been rounded over with a ³/16" radius router bit and the edge is marked for the dowel hole. Finger-gauge from each surface to quickly produce two marks at the approximate center. Drill at the center between these two marks.

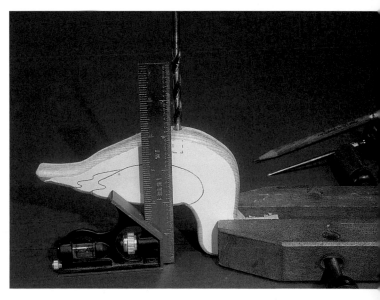

The piece is set up for drilling into the edge.

Carved Decoy Duck

SUPPLIES

1 1/8" to 1 1/2" pine: 5" x 10"

INSTRUCTIONS

1. Apply one Carved Decoy Duck pattern from page 133 to pine.

2. Cut the wood.

3. To carve a more realistic head and bill, use a center, pencil guideline drawn along the edges. This will help you keep the shape(s) symmetrical as you form it (see photo).

4. Coat some segments with a clear, natural finish and color others with acrylic paint before gluing them together.

5. Assemble and glue the segments.

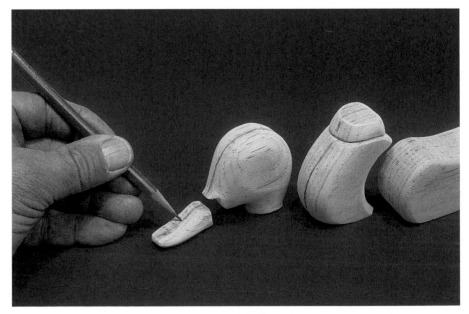

Pencil center lines along the edges as shown to help keep the shapes symmetrical if carving a more realistic head.

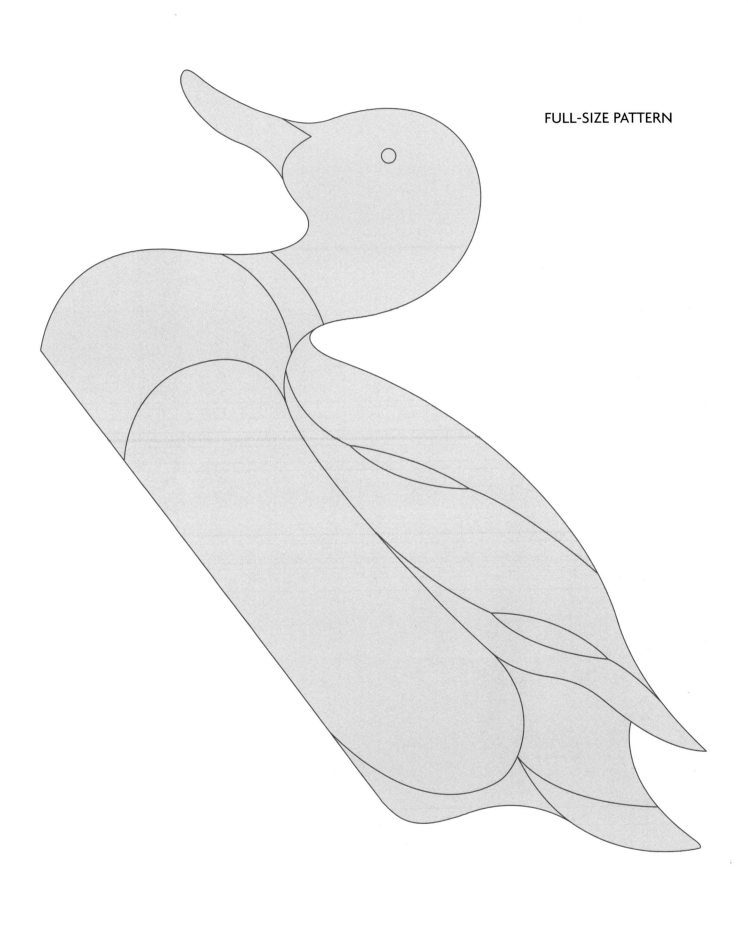

FULL-SIZE PATTERN

Striped Fish

Supplies
3/4" pine: 8" x 9 1/4"
1/8" to 1/4" plywood: 8" x 9 1/4"

INSTRUCTIONS

1. Apply one Striped Fish pattern from page 135 to plywood.

2. Cut the wood.

3. Smooth and shape the wood.

4. Color and finish the segments.

5. Assemble and glue the segments; make a backer.

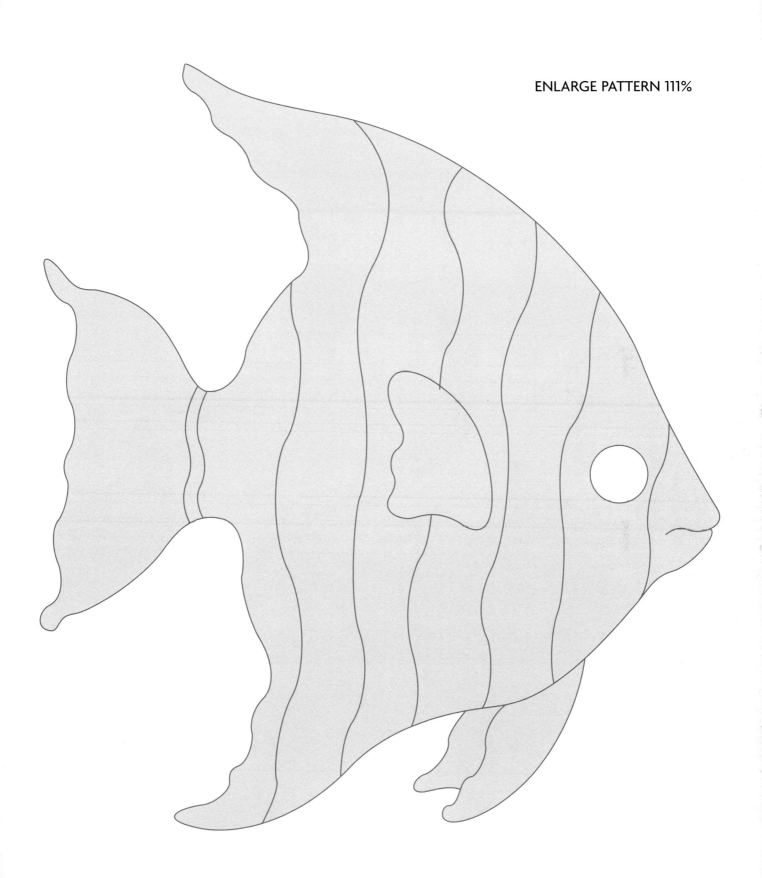

ENLARGE PATTERN 111%

Pink & Blue Fish

This fish design is made of thicker material to stand by itself without a plywood backer.

SUPPLIES

1 1/8" to 1 1/2" pine: 7" x 10"

INSTRUCTIONS

1. Apply one Pink & Blue Fish pattern from page 137 to plywood.

2. Cut the wood.

3. Smooth and shape the wood.

4. Color, finish and assemble the segments; make a backer.

Mermaid

SUPPLIES

3/4" clear pine: 7" x 9 3/8" for oval plaque
1/8" to 1/4" Baltic birch plywood: 4" x 8"
Sawtooth hanger

INSTRUCTIONS

1. Apply one Mermaid pattern from page 139 to Baltic birch plywood.

2. Cut the wood. Cut a 7" x 9 3/8" oval plaque from clear pine.

3. Round-over all edges about 1/16" radius.

4. Color and finish segments. Glue the segments, one at a time, directly onto the plaque.

5. Rope the plaque edge according to Making Rope-edged Plaques instructions on pages 125–127. An alternative is to rout a decorative edge around the plaque. Add a sawtooth hanger to the back.

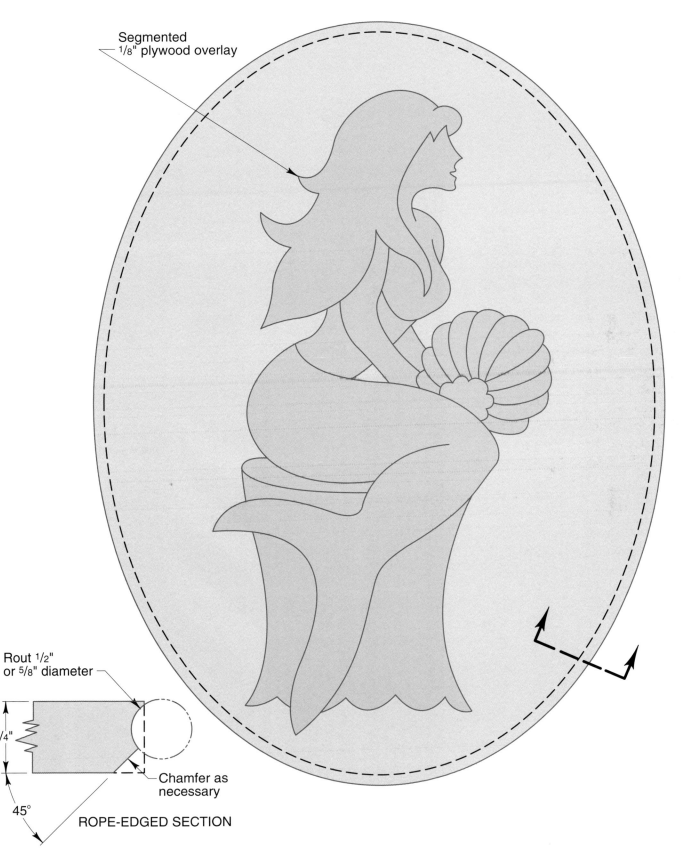

Segmented
1/8" plywood overlay

Rout 1/2"
or 5/8" diameter

3/4"

Chamfer as
necessary

45°

ROPE-EDGED SECTION

Cape Hatteras Lighthouse

A segmented version of North Carolina's Cape Hatteras Lighthouse, the tallest and one of the most famous lighthouses in America.

SUPPLIES

3/4" ash: 7" x 14 1/2" for plaque
3/4" clear pine: 4 1/4" x 13 1/4"
Sawtooth hanger

INSTRUCTIONS

1. Copy two Lighthouse patterns from pages 141–142. Apply one to ash for plaque. Cutting the other pattern horizontally with scissors, separate the main center tower section from the top and bottom. Apply the patterns for the top, center and bottom sections to clear pine in their respective positions.

2. Cut a 7" x 14 1/2" plaque from the ash. From the clear pine, cut out the central tower section as one complete unit (not individual segments).

3. Use a hand plane or a power abrasive tool to taper the central main tower from a thickness of 3/4" at the bottom to 1/2" at the top. Round over the edges of the main tower before reapplying the pattern to it with a temporary bonding spray adhesive.

4. Complete the cutting process, cutting the top, center, and bottom sections into all their segments. Reduce the segments to the appropriate thickness as specified on the pattern. Round over and/or chamfer the edges as appropriate.

5. Color and finish plaque and segments; glue the segments, one at a time, directly onto the plaque.

6. Rope the plaque edge according to Making Rope-edged Plaques instructions on pages 125–127. An alternative is to rout a decorative edge around the plaque. Attach a sawtooth hanger to the back.

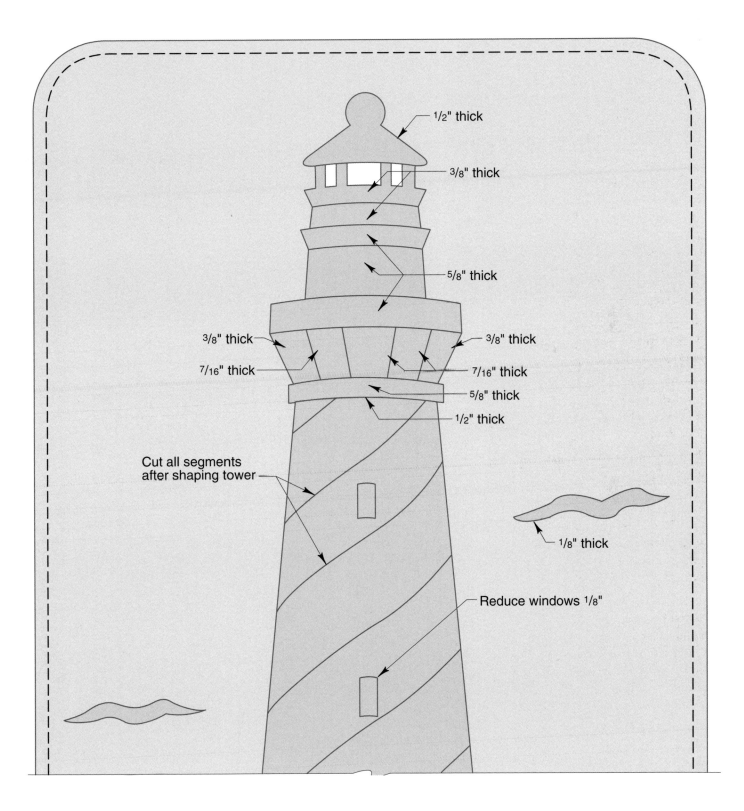

½" thick

³/₈" thick

⁵/₈" thick

³/₈" thick

³/₈" thick

⁷/₁₆" thick

⁷/₁₆" thick

⁵/₈" thick

½" thick

Cut all segments
after shaping tower

⅛" thick

Reduce windows ⅛"

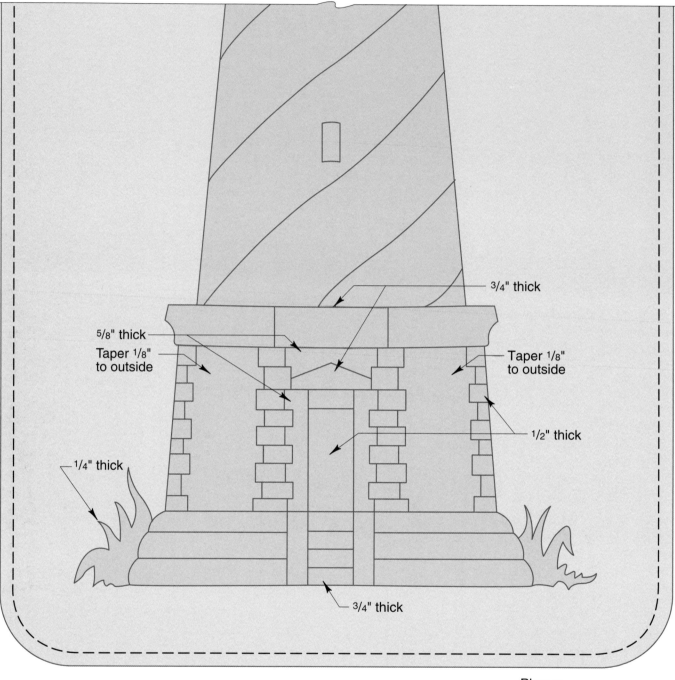

3/4" thick

5/8" thick

Taper 1/8"
to outside

Taper 1/8"
to outside

1/2" thick

1/4" thick

3/4" thick

Plaque
3/4" x 7" x 141/2"

Antique Anchor

SUPPLIES

3/4" clear pine: 7" x 9³/8" for oval plaque
3/4" straight-grained soft wood: 5³/4" x 7³/4"
Sawtooth hanger

INSTRUCTIONS

1. Apply one copy of Antique Anchor pattern from page 145 to clear pine, one copy to straight-grained soft wood.

2. Cut a 7" x 9³/8" oval plaque from clear pine. Cut the anchor shapes from the soft wood.

3. Reduce the thickness of segments as indicated on the pattern.

Note: Concentrating on one segment at a time makes round over work easier.

4. Chamfer the edges of the diamond-shaped segment to match those of the adjoining segments at the bottom.

Note: The segments are correctly shaped so that when assembled, the anchor appears to have a continuous v-groove carved down its center (see photos at right).

5. Shape the rope segments with carved v-grooves. Round over the corners by hand (see photo on page 144).

6. Glue anchor segments together one at a time prior to finishing.

7. Color and finish the plaque and assembled anchor. For a weathered look, use a three-step, water-based green patina finish. For directions, see page 11.

8. Glue the assembled, finished anchor segments directly onto the plaque. Rope the plaque edge according to Making Rope-edged Plaques instructions on page 125–127. An alternative is to rout a decorative edge around the plaque. Attach a sawtooth hanger to the back.

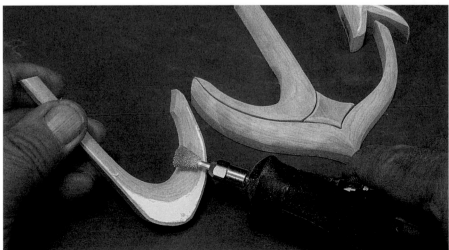

Shape a segment of the Anchor using a rotary tool with a structured carbide cutter.

Design Tip

As an option, you can choose to omit the segments of hand-carved rope. In this case, change the pattern so it has a complete ring at the top.

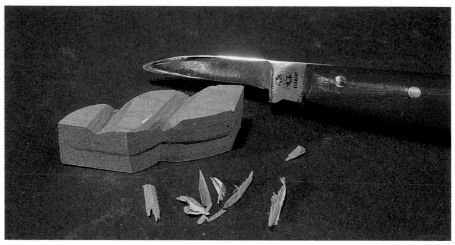

Shape the carved rope beginning with a series of slanted knife cuts to make v-grooves.

The Anchor carving is complete. Glue the Anchor segments together prior to finishing.

The first step to a metallic patina finish is to apply liquid copper (or brass) finish over a sealer.

The patina solution, applied with a sponge, changes the look of the copper.

ENLARGE PATTERN 111%

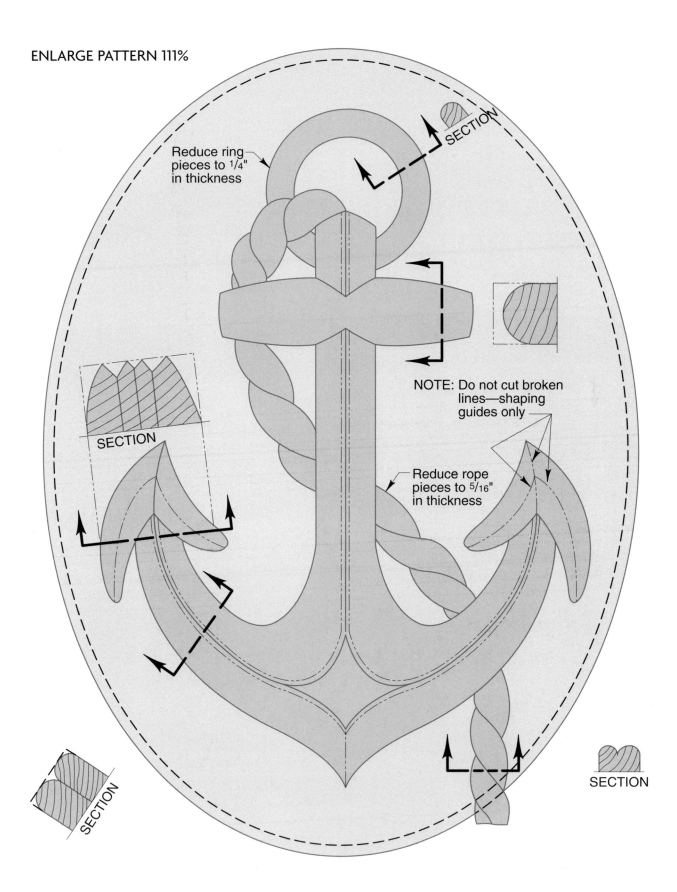

Reduce ring pieces to $1/4$" in thickness

SECTION

NOTE: Do not cut broken lines—shaping guides only

SECTION

Reduce rope pieces to $5/16$" in thickness

SECTION

SECTION

Sculpted Sailboat

Supplies

3/4" ash: 7" x 9 3/8" for oval plaque

7/8" pine: 5" x 6 1/4"; 1" x 5"

Sawtooth hanger

INSTRUCTIONS

1. Apply one Sculpted Sailboat pattern from page 147 to pine, one to ash.

2. Cut a 7" x 9 3/8" oval from ash.

3. Rough-shape all boat segments first by compound-sawing them (see photo). Carefully remove the profile pattern after compound-sawing. Round-over the front sail.

4. Reapply the pattern and cut out the segments.

5. Color, finish and assemble the segments.

6. Rope the plaque edge according to Making Rope-edged Plaques instructions on pages 125–127. An alternative is to rout a decorative edge around the plaque. Attach a sawtooth hanger to the back.

Right: Rough-cut segments to shape by compound-sawing with the scroll saw and/or with the help of a disk or belt sander.

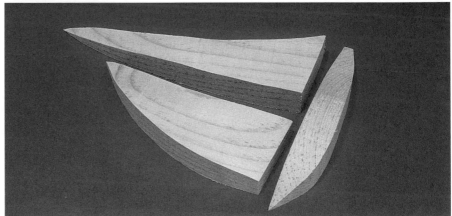

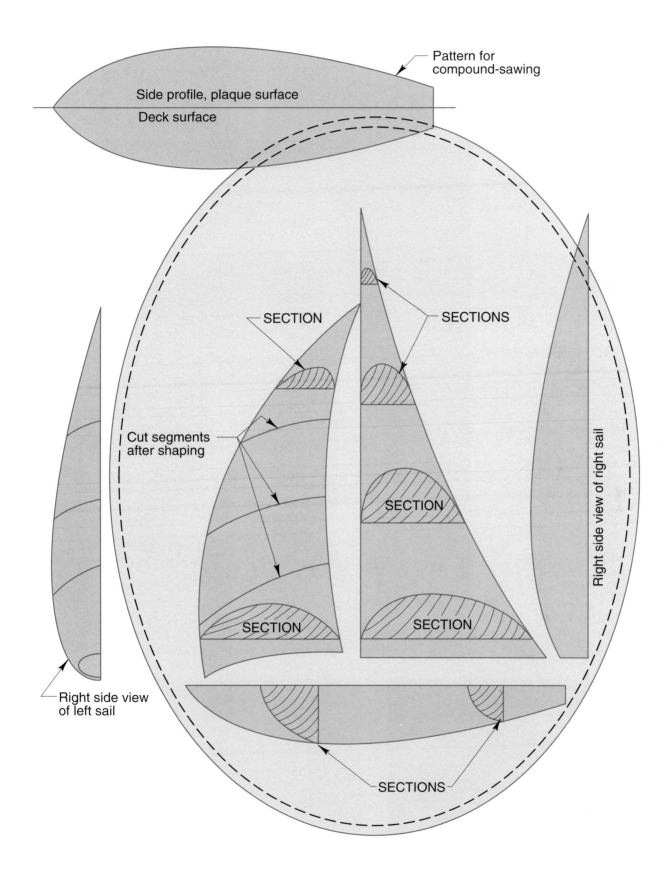

Pattern for compound-sawing

Side profile, plaque surface

Deck surface

SECTION

SECTIONS

Cut segments after shaping

SECTION

Right side view of right sail

SECTION

SECTION

SECTION

Right side view of left sail

SECTIONS

Favorites
First Kiss

SUPPLIES

$7/8$" to $1 1/8$" pine: 6" x 16"

$3/4$" pine: 2" x $9 1/2$"

INSTRUCTIONS

1. Apply one First Kiss pattern from page 149 to large piece of pine.

2. Cut the wood.

3. Round-over all edges.

4. Use a wood-burning tool to texture the boy's hair (see photo, below left).

5. Color, finish and assemble the segments; make a backer.

6. Cut mortises into the base as indicated. Insert the scroll-sawn tenons into mortises cut into the base (see photo, below right).

Below: The boy's hair segment is tapered toward the top and then textured with a wood-burning tool.

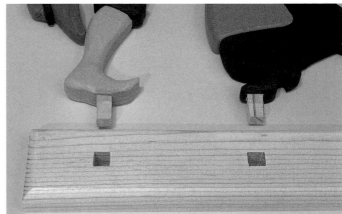

Mortises and tenons are cut with a scroll saw to support the figures on a simple base.

ENLARGE 182% FOR FULL-SIZE PATTERN

NOTE:
Where thickness reduction is required, it is indicated by a minus (-) sign before the amount to be reduced.

-1/8"
-1/4"
-1/8"
-1/8"
-1/8"
-1/8"
-1/8"
-1/4"
-1/8"
-1/8"
-1/8"

3/8" square tenons

3/8"R

Base: 3/4" x 2" x 91/2"

Rooster Plaques

SUPPLIES

3/4" pine: 11" x 15"; 10 1/2" x 15"

1/8" to 1/4" plywood: 11" x 15"; 10 1/2" x 15"

INSTRUCTIONS

1. Apply a Rooster Plaques pattern from page 151 or 152 to pine.

2. Cut the wood.

3. Round over all edges about 3/16" radius. If desired, reduce the thickness of the feet, the combs, and the wattles (under the beak) 3/16".

4. Color, finish and assemble the segments; make a backer.

ENLARGE PATTERN 200%

ENLARGE PATTERN 200%

Carved Mirror

SUPPLIES

3/4" butternut: 8 1/2" x 10 1/4"

1/8" to 1/4" acrylic mirror: 6 1/2" x 8"

INSTRUCTIONS

1. Apply one Carved Mirror pattern from page 154 to butternut.

2. Cut the wood.

3. Round-over the edges, following the small arrows on the petals of the flower in the pattern, suggesting an optional tapering toward the center.

4. Apply a coat of nongloss water-based poly-urethane.

5. Assemble the segments and make a backer.

6. Use the backer to mark the shape on the mirror (see photo, below right).

Note: A ballpoint pen will mark the front of the mirror. There is no protective covering on the back-side, so it is very important to avoid scratching it.

7. Cut out the mirror.

Note: It is best to use a piece of lightweight cardboard under the acrylic to protect it during cutting. Hold cardboard in place with masking tape pulled over onto the front of the mirror. Do not allow the tape to come in contact with the mirror backing as it may pull off the reflective coating when removed.

8. Insert the mirror and secure it to the wood with a small bead of adhesive.

Right: Using the plywood backer as a pattern, lay out the cutting line for the acrylic mirror.

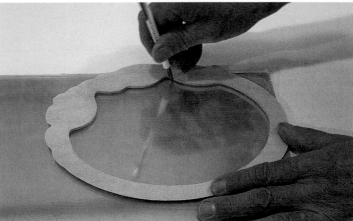

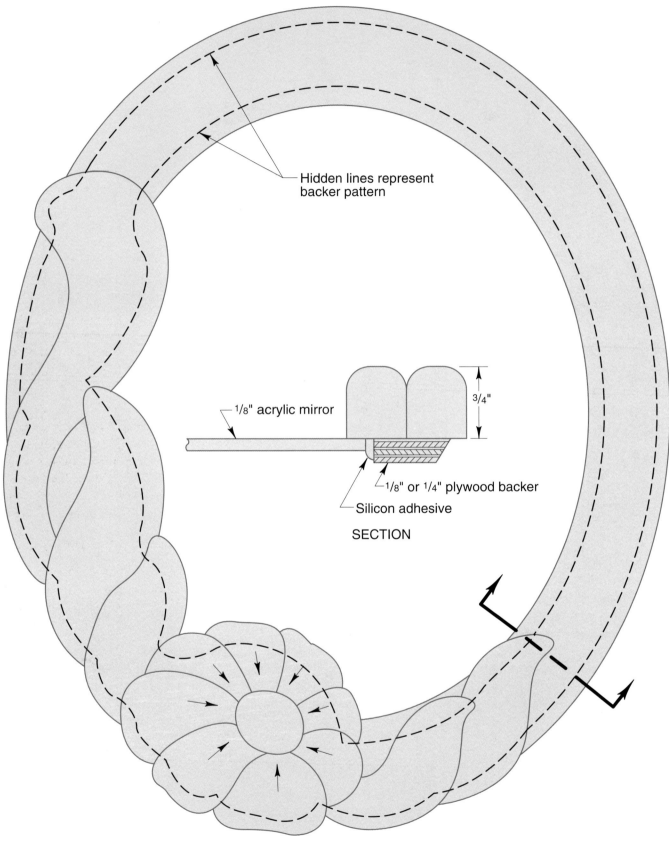

Hidden lines represent
backer pattern

3/4"

1/8" acrylic mirror

1/8" or 1/4" plywood backer

Silicon adhesive

SECTION

Segmented Sunflower

SUPPLIES

3/4" pine: 9" x 26 1/4"

1/8" plywood: 9" x 26 1/4"

INSTRUCTIONS

1. Apply one Segmented Sunflower pattern from pages 156–157 to pine.

2. Cut the wood. Leave the pattern paper on the wood until sanding, to indicate the face or upper side of the segments.

3. Notice that the pattern has two lines around the center of the flower. Cut on the outer line around the center of the flower; sand to the inside line, reducing the size of the center segment.

Note: This will allow the surrounding petals to slide in further toward the center and thus reduce open gaps resulting from the many saw kerfs made when cutting out all of the petal segments.

4. Shape and smooth the wood. Use imagination and intuition when shaping the petals. Most should taper in thickness inward toward the center of the flower. Give all petals (with the exception of the four "A" petals) a sideways slant. See the petal shaping sketches on the Segmented Sunflower pattern on opposite page.

Reduce the four "B" petals to 1/2" thickness. Round-over all edges of the petals to 1/8" radius. Round-over the edges of the center of the segment to 3/8" radius.

5. Taper the stem from 3/4" thickness at the bottom to 1/2" where it meets the petals. Leave one edge sharp on each of the leaf segments and round-over the other edge to 3/8" radius. See the Segmented Sunflower pattern on page 157. Reduce the remaining segments of each leaf to 1/2" thickness and round-over all edges to 1/4" radius.

6. Color, finish and assemble the segments; make a backer.

ENLARGE 117% FOR FULL-SIZE PATTERN

NOTE: Reduce "B" petals to 1/2" in thickness

B

B

A

Cut on outside line,
sand to inside line

A

B

A

A

A

B

"A" petals

Double slant

Typical petal shapes
before rounding over

A ———— A

1/8" plywood backing

Typical section through
center of flower

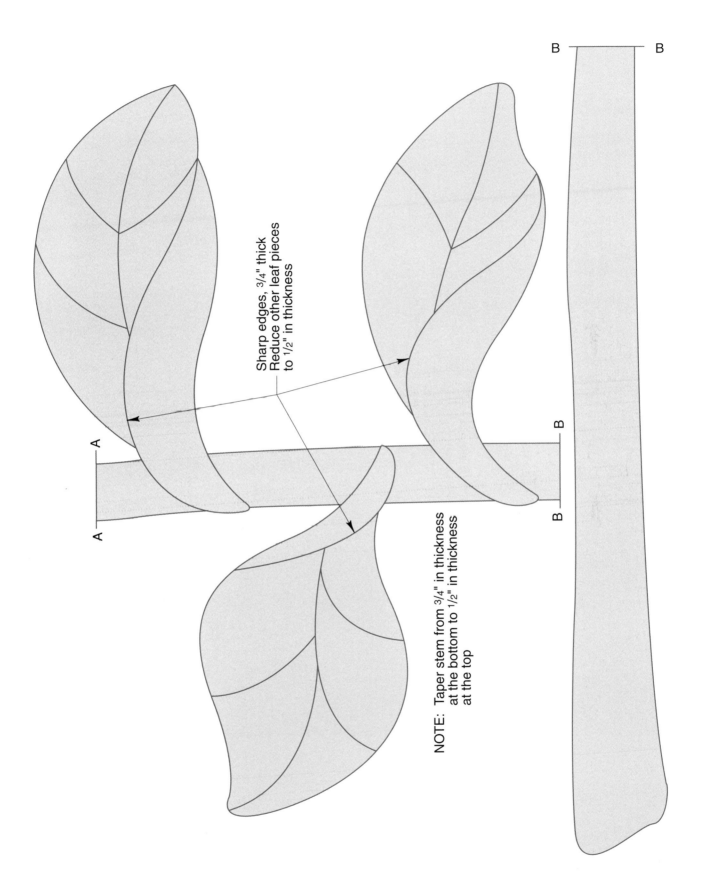

Sharp edges, 3/4" thick
Reduce other leaf pieces
to 1/2" in thickness

NOTE: Taper stem from 3/4" in thickness
at the bottom to 1/2" in thickness
at the top

Monarch Butterfly

SUPPLIES

3/4" pine: 3/4" x 4"

1/8" plywood: 6 1/2" x 7" (2)

Wire: 16 gauge

INSTRUCTIONS

1. Apply one Monarch Butterfly pattern from pages 160–161 to each piece of plywood.

2. Cut the wood.

3. Make the 12° beveled surfaces as shown on the Monarch Butterfly pattern on page 161 for the bottom of the body.

4. Cut out the rough shape, using the body compound-sawing patterns (see photo, opposite top).

5. Simultaneously stack-cut the right and left wing. Save the scraps for stack-cutting the overlays.

6. Round over the corners to shape the upper surfaces of the body, using a drum sander (see photo, opposite center).

7. Round over and slightly contour the wing edges (see photo, opposite below). Round over the overlay edges.

8. Drill holes in the body for the wire antennae. Shape the wires and glue them in place.

9. Color and finish the segments. Once the paint has dried, add dots for detail.

Note: An easy way to do this is by using the pointed handle end of a small paintbrush or a tooth-pick dipped into the paint. Make the dots just as you would use a pen or pencil to dot the letter "i." Frequently remove excess paint from the handle so it does not build up and make progressively larger dots.

10. Assemble the segments. Glue the body to the wings. See Monarch Butterfly pattern on next page and end view of the bottom of the body. Make a backer.

11. Drill a small hole, angled slightly upwards, only part-way into the back to hang the completed piece on a nail.

Above: The butterfly body is cut to rough shape by employing compound scroll sawing techniques. Notice the pattern is centered on the two beveled surfaces.

Right: After compound sawing, round over the corners to give shape to the upper surfaces of the body. The wings are then glued to the flat beveled surfaces.

Below: Shape the edges and surfaces of the 1/8" plywood segment overlays with coarse abrasive paper.

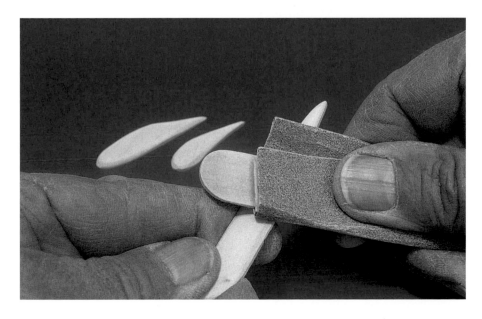

FULL-SIZE PATTERN

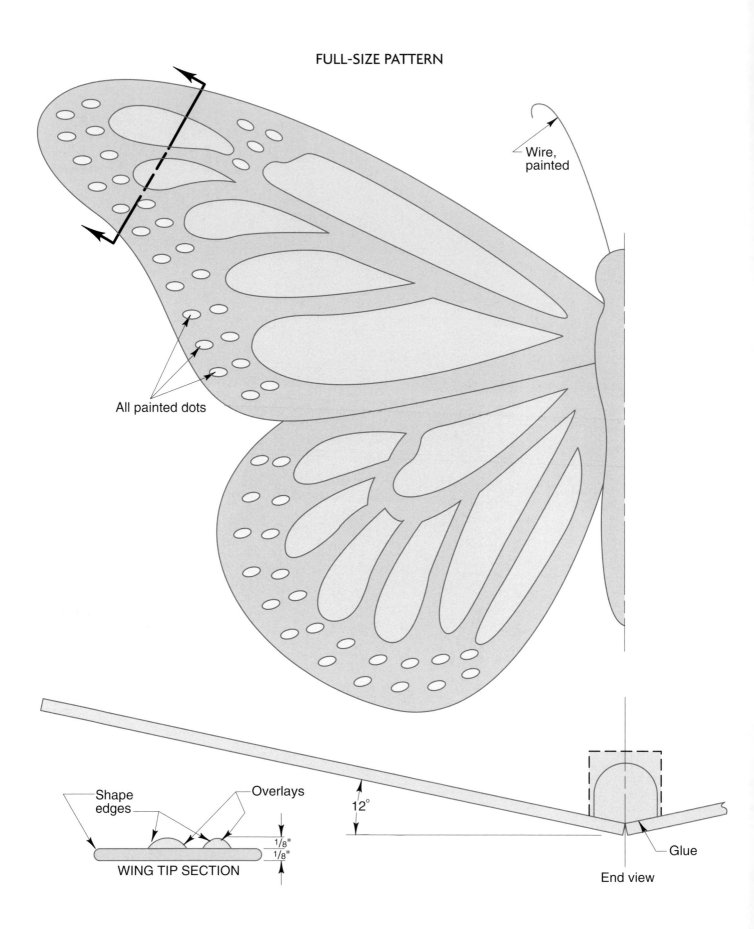

Wire, painted

All painted dots

Shape edges

Overlays

1/8"
1/8"

WING TIP SECTION

12°

Glue

End view

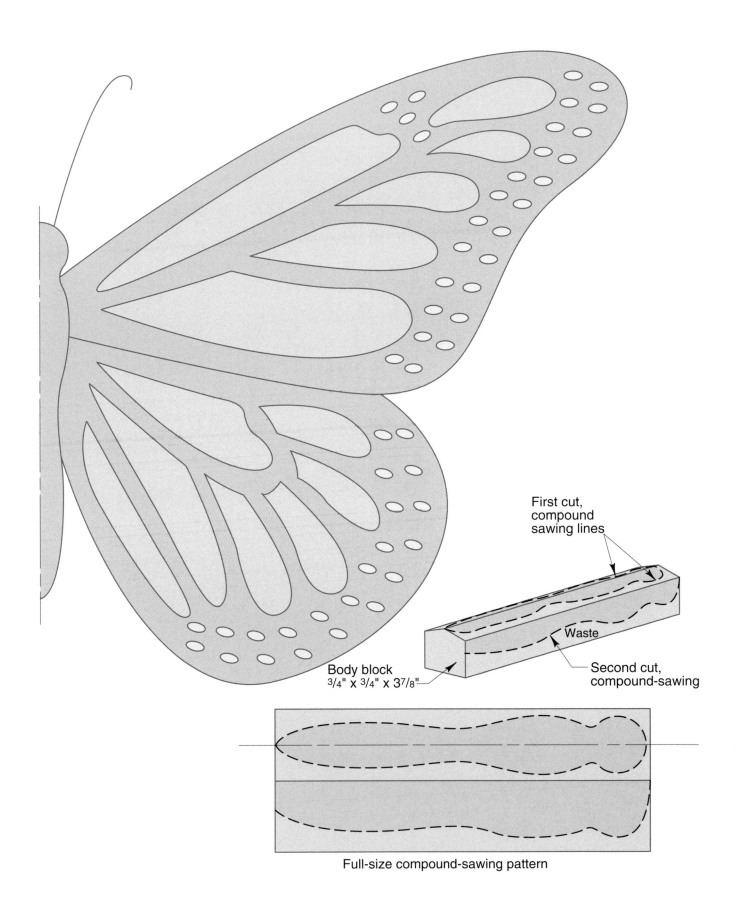

First cut,
compound
sawing lines

Waste

Second cut,
compound-sawing

Body block
3/4" x 3/4" x 3⁷/8"

Full-size compound-sawing pattern

Swan

SUPPLIES

3/4" MDF (medium density fiberboard): 11" x 14 3/4"

1/8" to 1/4" plywood: 11" x 14 3/4"

INSTRUCTIONS

1. Apply one Swan pattern from page 163 to MDF.

2. Cut the MDF.

3. Round over the edges of all segments except the flower segments.

4. Give convex surfaces to flower segments with a small drum sander (see photo, below).

5. Color, finish, and assemble the segments; make a backer.

Above: A 3/4" diameter drum sander is used to give convex shapes to the flower petals.

Above, right: The flower petal shaping is shown here in progress.

Right: Here, all segments are shaped and ready to be painted. Note the small router used to round-over the edges. After painting, the segments will be glued together edge to edge, using the second photocopy of the pattern.

ENLARGE 167% FOR FULL-SIZE PATTERN

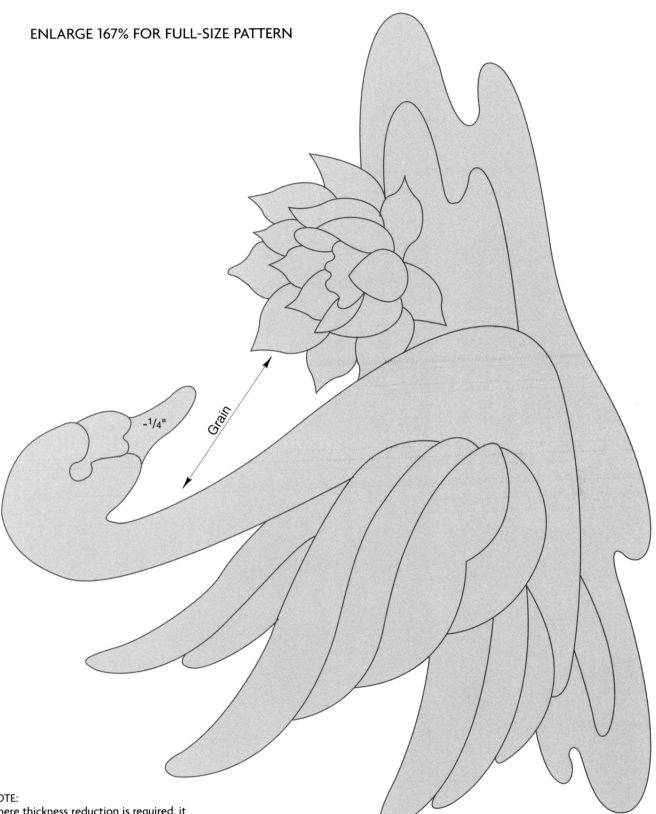

NOTE:
Where thickness reduction is required, it is indicated by a minus (-) sign before the amount to be reduced.

Segmented Pony

SUPPLIES

3/4" pine: 10" x 17"

1/8" to 1/4" plywood: 10" x 17"

INSTRUCTIONS

1. Apply one Segmented Pony pattern from page 165 to pine.

2. Cut the wood.

3. Reduce the thickness of segments indicated with a minus sign (-) on the pattern.

4. Using a belt or disc sander, shape the grassy leaves by beveling and/or tapering the front surfaces in various directions, following arrows on the pattern that indicate the recommended direction of slope.

5. Round over all edges 1/16" to 1/8" radius. Finish-sand all segments, using 150- or 180-grit sand paper.

6. Apply a coat of clear polyurethane or acrylic finish to all segments.

7. Assemble the segments; make a backer.

NOTE:
Where thickness reduction is required, it is indicated by a minus (-) sign before the amount to be reduced.

An arrow (⟶) indicates bevel/tapering direction.

Unicorn

SUPPLIES

3/4" MDF (medium density fiberboard) or solid wood: 12" x 16"

1/8" to 1/4" plywood: 12" x 16"

INSTRUCTIONS

1. Apply one Unicorn pattern from page 168 to wood.

2. Cut the wood.

3. Reduce the inner ear thickness 1/4" and do not round its edges.

4. Round over all other segments about 1/4" or 5/16" radius, except the inner eye, which is about 1/8" radius (see photos, opposite).

5. Sand all segments; paint the inner ear gray before assembly. Assemble and glue all the rest of the segments edge to edge before painting (see photo, opposite lower right).

6. Make a backer. Paint the entire project: inside of the nostril and the eye black; the horn gold, then apply some gold or silver glitter, if desired.

Design Tip

If making the Unicorn from solid wood, make it from two pieces: one 3/4" x 1 1/2" x 7" for the horn, and another piece 3/4" x 12" x 12" for the head. See recommended grain orientation for solid wood construction given on the Unicorn pattern on page 168.

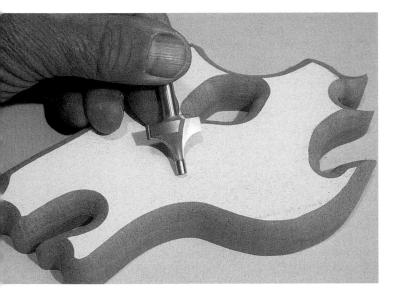

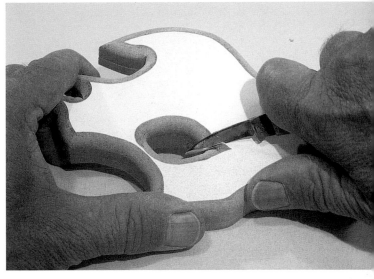

Above: This carbide-tipped router bit with its very small pilot (just 5/32" diameter) is ideal for getting into tight corners.

Above, right: Use a knife to round the edges of the inside corner of the Unicorn's eye.

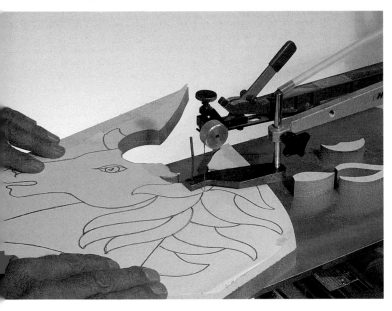

Above: Cut the Unicorn into segments.

Right: All shaping to the individual segments is completed. The project is now ready for assembly and painting.

Sun Face

SUPPLIES

3/4" butternut: 8" x 8"
1/8" to 1/4" plywood: 8" x 8"

INSTRUCTIONS

1. Apply one Sun Face pattern from page 171 to butternut. Mount the pattern so the wood grain runs vertically.

2. Cut the wood.

3. Reduce the thickness of those segments marked with a minus sign (-) on the patterns (see photos on next page).

4. Carefully work those segments with short vertical grain, especially the upper lip of the Sun Face. Use a coarse-grit drum sander with light pressure to remove stock quickly without fracturing the delicate tips.

5. Make shims for the cheeks, nose, eyebrows, and chin of the Sun Face.

6. Sand all segments carefully, removing all cross-grain scratches resulting from coarse abrasives.

7. Paint the eye segments white with black (refer to photo, right).

8. Apply a clear, nongloss finish and assemble the segments; make a backer.

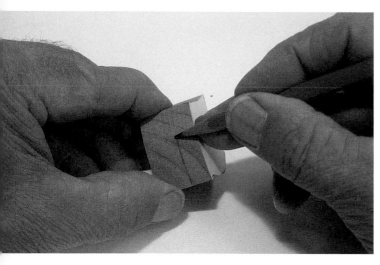

Finger-gauge a guide line for reducing the thickness. Notice that the paper pattern is still attached to the facing surface of the wood. Always remove stock from face surfaces, not from backs.

The perimeter segments of the Sun Face have been reduced in thickness. Not all edges of all segments are rounded over. Here, a pencil mark indicates where the rounding over of a higher adjacent segment should begin.

A small, high-speed rotary tool, fitted with a coarse-grit drum sander, makes edge rounding easy.

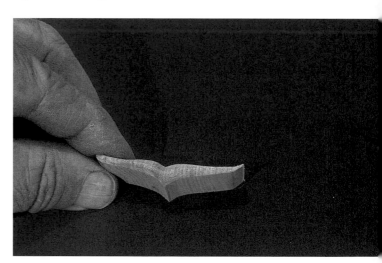

The upper lip of Sun Face has "short grain," which must be worked very carefully so it does not fracture.

After the segments have been glued back together at the edges, trace the outline on 1/8" or 1/4" plywood backer material.

NOTE:
Where thickness reduction is required, it is indicated by a minus (-) sign before the amount to be reduced.

A plus (+) sign indicates segments to be shimmed.

Moon Face

SUPPLIES

3/4" butternut: 8" x 8"

1/8" to 1/4" plywood: 8" x 8"

INSTRUCTIONS

1. Apply one Moon Face pattern from page 174 to butternut. Mount the pattern so the wood grain runs vertically.

2. Cut the wood.

3. Shape and Smooth the wood. Reduce the thickness of those segments marked with a minus sign (-) on the patterns.

3. Carefully work those segments with short vertical grain. Use a coarse-grit drum sander with light pressure to remove stock quickly without fracturing the delicate tips.

4. Make a 1/8" shim for the cheek of the Moon Face (see photo, below right).

5. Taper the surface of the Moon Face from the nose toward the cap from 3/4" to about 1/2" in thickness. Taper the cap from 3/4" to about 1/4" at the juncture of the vertical ribbon segment that will be attached to the star.

6. Sand all segments carefully, removing all cross-grain scratches resulting from coarse abrasives.

7. Assemble all segments, gluing them together edge to edge, except for the ribbon and star segments.

8. Make a backer. Glue the ribbon and star segments on after the backer has been glued in place. Apply a clear, nongloss finish.

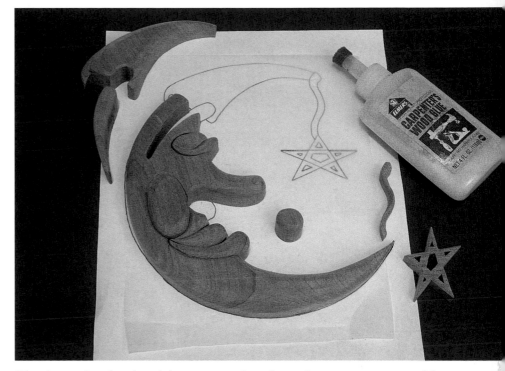

Glue the cut, shaped, and sanded segments together, edge to edge, over an extra copy of the pattern. Note the waxed paper protecting the pattern.

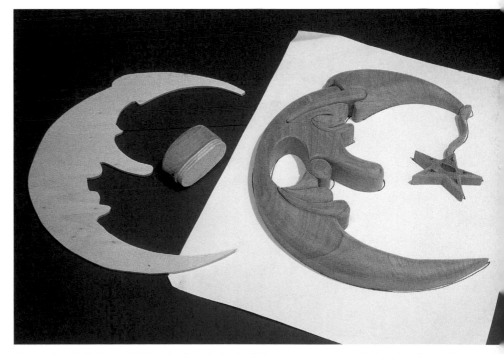

Notice the 1/8" plywood shim glued to the back of the cheek segment, and that the plywood backer at the left does not include backing support for the star or hanging ribbon segments.

FULL-SIZE PATTERN

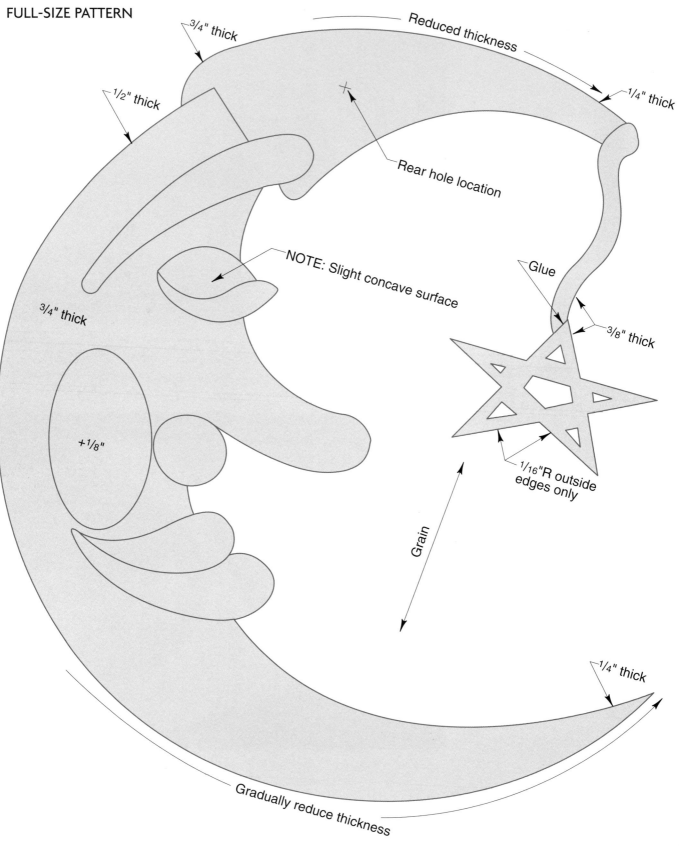

3/4" thick

1/2" thick

Reduced thickness

1/4" thick

Rear hole location

Glue

3/8" thick

NOTE: Slight concave surface

3/4" thick

+1/8"

1/16"R outside edges only

Grain

1/4" thick

Gradually reduce thickness

Seasonal & Spiritual
Pumpkin & Ghost

SUPPLIES

3/4"-thick MDF: 8 1/2" x 9 3/4" for pumpkin; 6 1/2" x 11 1/2" for ghost
1/8"-thick plywood: 8 1/2" x 9 3/4" for pumpkin backer

INSTRUCTIONS

1. Apply one Pumpkin & Ghost pattern from page 176 to MDF (medium density fiberboard).

2. Cut the wood.

3. Reduce the stem and leaf segments to 1/2" thickness. Slightly round over the leaf and stem segments. Round over the pumpkin segments and ghost profiles to 5/16" radius.

4. Color, finish and assemble the segments, and make a backer.

5. Coil two pieces of the green electrical wire. Drill holes in the stem segment for the wire curls and glue them in place.

Design Tip

The ghost can be temporarily attached to the back of the pumpkin with double-sided tape. After Halloween, remove the ghost and the pumpkin alone can be used as a Thanksgiving decoration.

Holiday Turkey

This Thanksgiving wall plaque involves basic techniques. In addition to reducing the thickness of some segments as indicated on the pattern, the two central wing segments are shimmed and the feathers taper from 3/4" in thickness at the tips to 3/8" where they meet the body.

SUPPLIES

3/4"-thick MDF (medium density fiberboard): 9 3/4" x 13"
1/8"- to 1/4"-thick plywood: 9 3/4" x 13"

INSTRUCTIONS

1. Apply one Holiday Turkey pattern from page 178 to MDF.

2. Cut the Wood.

3. Reduce the thickness of those segments indicated with a minus (-) sign on the drawing. Remember, it is best to remove material from the front rather than the back.

4. Cut shims 1/8" and 1/4" thick to elevate the wing segments marked with a plus (+) on the pattern.

5. Taper the tail feather segments inward toward the body using a disc or belt sander.

Note: Not all segments are rounded over, such as the edges of the tail feathers where they butt to the body (see photo, below left). These, and the edges of thinner segments not rounded over, are indicated with a small "V" mark on the pattern.

6. Color, finish, and assemble the segments; make a backer.

Left: Not all edges are rounded over, such as these thinner segments that butt to a thicker or shimmed segment.

ENLARGE 150% FOR FULL-SIZE PATTERN

Round-over feather segments
and beak separation
1/16"R

-1/4"   -1/4"

-1/4"

+1/4"

+1/8"

-3/8"   -1/4"

-1/2"   -3/8"

NOTE: Round-over all edges 1/4" or 5/16"R
except those noted:
< Denotes edges not rounded over
- Indicates thickness reduction
+ Indicates shim to increase thickness

Santa Face

SUPPLIES

3/4"-thick pine: 8 1/2" x 6 3/4"

1/8" to 1/4" plywood: 8 1/2" x 6 3/4"

INSTRUCTIONS

1. Apply one Santa Face pattern from page 180 to pine.

2. Cut the wood.

3. Round over all edges 1/4" radius.

4. Apply red aniline stain or red acrylic paint to the cap, nose, and lower mouth segments. Apply a natural finish to the cheeks and upper mouth. Paint the right segments on both eyes black. Dot the eyes with white paint. Apply a whitewash to all other segments by wiping on a thinned white acrylic paint.

5. Assemble the segments; make a backer.

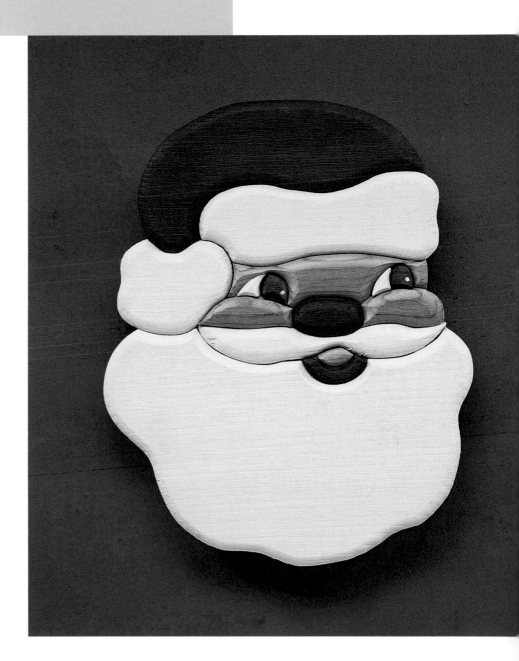

Angel

SUPPLIES

1/2" ash (or any other nicely grained wood): 8 1/4" x 17 1/2"

1/8"- to 1/4"-thick plywood: 8 1/4" x 17 1/2"

INSTRUCTIONS

1. Apply one Heavenly Angel pattern from page 182 to ash.

2. Cut the wood.

3. Chamfer all edges about 1/16" to 1/8".

4. Finish this project so some of the wood figure, or grain, shows through. Paint each segment with a coat of acrylic paint thinned with water, then wipe it off immediately with a paper towel or cotton rag.

5. Assemble the segments; make a backer (see photos, next page).

Assemble the pre-finished segments, gluing them edge to edge over a second copy of the pattern protected with waxed paper.

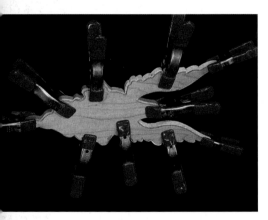

Use spring clamps to hold the backer to the pre-glued segments.

Nativity

SUPPLIES

3/4"-thick clear ash: 8 3/4" x 12"
1/8"- to 1/4"-thick plywood: 8 3/8" x 12"

INSTRUCTIONS

1. Apply one Nativity pattern from page 184 to pine.

2. Cut the wood. Drill small blade-threading holes; one at an inside frame corner and one along the bottom edge of the child's face.

3. Chamfer the edges.

4. Color and finish the segments.

Note: *Do not attempt to glue the segments together edge to edge as is the usual practice.* Because of the integral frame cut around all the segments, large gaps between segments may result unless you use precautions in assembly, due to the accumulation of space resulting from the many saw kerfs. Instead, prepare the plywood backer and glue the cut and finished frame to it. Only after the glued frame has set should the remaining pre-finished segments be glued down, keeping equal gaps between the segments with small cardboard spacers (see photos, below).

Because of the surrounding frame and many saw kerfs, excessive space may result unless all segments are spaced evenly.

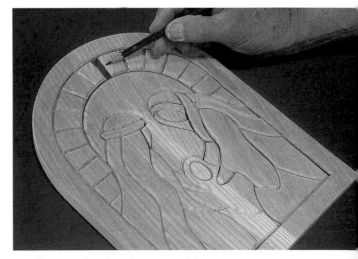

Small pieces of cardboard are inserted between segments to space them uniformly as they are glued to a plywood backer.

Madonna & Child

SUPPLIES

3/4"-thick poplar: 7 1/4" x 13"
1/8" to 1/4" plywood: 7 1/4" x 13 1/4"

INSTRUCTIONS

1. Apply one Madonna & Child pattern from page 186 to poplar.

2. Cut the wood.

3. Chamfer all the edges.

4. Color the segments with various colored oil stains. Coat the entire project with one or more coats of a non-gloss, clear finish.

5. Assemble the segments; make a backer.

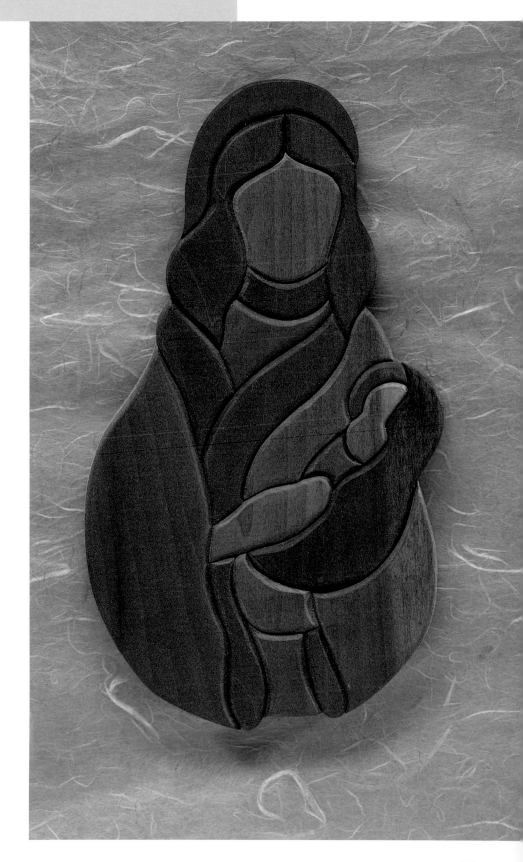

Metric Equivalency Chart

MM-MILLIMETRES   **CM-CENTIMETRES**

INCHES TO MILLIMETRES AND CENTIMETRES

INCHES	MM	CM	INCHES	CM	INCHES	CM
⅛	3	0.3	9	22.9	30	76.2
¼	6	0.6	10	25.4	31	78.7
⅜	10	1.0	11	27.9	32	81.3
½	13	1.3	12	30.5	33	83.8
⅝	16	1.6	13	33.0	34	86.4
¾	19	1.9	14	35.6	35	88.9
⅞	22	2.2	15	38.1	36	91.4
1	25	2.5	16	40.6	37	94.0
1 ¼	32	3.2	17	43.2	38	96.5
1 ½	38	3.8	18	45.7	39	99.1
1 ¾	44	4.4	19	48.3	40	101.6
2	51	5.1	20	50.8	41	104.1
2 ½	64	6.4	21	53.3	42	106.7
3	76	7.6	22	55.9	43	109.2
3 ½	89	8.9	23	58.4	44	111.8
4	102	10.2	24	61.0	45	114.3
4 ½	114	11.4	25	63.5	46	116.8
5	127	12.7	26	66.0	47	119.4
6	152	15.2	27	68.6	48	121.9
7	178	17.8	28	71.1	49	124.5
8	203	20.3	29	73.7	50	127.0

YARDS TO METRES

YARDS	METRES	YARDS	METRES	YARDS	METRES	YARDS	METRES	YARDS	METRES
⅛	0.11	2 ⅛	1.94	4 ⅛	3.77	6 ⅛	5.60	8 ⅛	7.43
¼	0.23	2 ¼	2.06	4 ¼	3.89	6 ¼	5.72	8 ¼	7.54
⅜	0.34	2 ⅜	2.17	4 ⅜	4.00	6 ⅜	5.83	8 ⅜	7.66
½	0.46	2 ½	2.29	4 ½	4.11	6 ½	5.94	8 ½	7.77
⅝	0.57	2 ⅝	2.40	4 ⅝	4.23	6 ⅝	6.06	8 ⅝	7.89
¾	0.69	2 ¾	2.51	4 ¾	4.34	6 ¾	6.17	8 ¾	8.00
⅞	0.80	2 ⅞	2.63	4 ⅞	4.46	6 ⅞	6.29	8 ⅞	8.12
1	0.91	3	2.74	5	4.57	7	6.40	9	8.23
1 ⅛	1.03	3 ⅛	2.86	5 ⅛	4.69	7 ⅛	6.52	9 ⅛	8.34
1 ¼	1.14	3 ¼	2.97	5 ¼	4.80	7 ¼	6.63	9 ¼	8.46
1 ⅜	1.26	3 ⅜	3.09	5 ⅜	4.91	7 ⅜	6.74	9 ⅜	8.57
1 ½	1.37	3 ½	3.20	5 ½	5.03	7 ½	6.86	9 ½	8.69
1 ⅝	1.49	3 ⅝	3.31	5 ⅝	5.14	7 ⅝	6.97	9 ⅝	8.80
1 ¾	1.60	3 ¾	3.43	5 ¾	5.26	7 ¾	7.09	9 ¾	8.92
1 ⅞	1.71	3 ⅞	3.54	5 ⅞	5.37	7 ⅞	7.20	9 ⅞	9.03
2	1.83	4	3.66	6	5.49	8	7.32	10	9.14

Index

Extended Credits and Rights Information
(continued from p. 4)

The publishers of *The Pattern Companion: Scroll Saw* gratefully acknowledges permission for the use of material designated below from the following previously published works:

Decorative & Ornamental Scroll Saw Patterns, by Patrick Spielman & Dirk Boelman
© 2000, Patrick Spielman & Dirk Boelman; information and projects from pages:
5-14, 19-27, 29-33, 40-52, 54, 56, 60, 62-92, 98-105, 112-125

Scroll Saw Art, by Patrick Spielman & Kerry Shirts © 2000, Chapelle Ltd.
Information and projects from pages:
19-31, 34-39, 42-49, 54-55, 58-59, 63, 70-73, 76-81, 84-87, 99-102

Scroll Saw Segmentation, by Patrick Spielman © 2000, Chapelle Ltd.
Information and projects from pages:
6–7, 14–32, 35-40, 43-44, 49-86, 93-100, 104-105, 109-112, 127

Photographs appearing in this book on page 5 (top) and between pages 10-83
were supplied by Patrick Spielman and Dirk Boelman;
those on pages 3, 5 (center and bottom), 7-8, 89-186
are by Kevin Dilley for Hazen Photography